A Guidebook to

Ethnic Vancouver

Walking, Shopping, and Eating Tours of the Ethnic Neighborhoods of Vancouver

Anne Petrie

Illustrations by

Barb Wood

hancock
house

ISBN 0-88839-159-5

Copyright © 1982 Anne Petrie

Cataloging in Publication Data

Petrie, Anne
  A guidebook to ethnic Vancouver

1. Vancouver (B.C.) — Population
Ethnic Groups. 2.Vancouver (B.C.) —
Stores, shopping centers, etc. 3. Van-
couver (B.C.) — Restaurants. I. Title.
FC3847.9.A1P47   971.1'33004   C82-091234-4
F1089.5.V22P47

Editor Kelly Allen
Typeset by Lisa Smedman & Verlee Webb in Times Roman
  on an AM Varityper Comp/Edit
Production, Layout & Cover Design Crystal Ryan
Illustrations by Barb Wood
Printed in Canada by Friesen Printers

Cover Photo P. Munro

2nd edition 1983

Hancock House Publishers Ltd.
19313 Zero Avenue, Surrey, B.C., Canada V3S 5J9

Hancock House Publishers
1431 Harrison Avenue, Blaine, WA 98230

TABLE OF CONTENTS

Olivieri's, at Commercial & 3rd

PREFACE

I remember the summer afternoon I first visited Little Italy. I had determined to spend my vacation exploring my own city, Vancouver, and my first stop was Commercial Drive. Going in and out of the stores, I knew that this was a special area of town and I loved it already. But at the same time I was also aware that there was a lot here that I didn't understand. The selection of pasta shapes intimidated me, and as far as cheese went, after parmesan, I was lost. And what were you supposed to do with those big pieces of dried fish? Were those boxed cakes hanging from the ceiling for some special occasion I didn't know about?

I suppose that was the day this book really began. Wouldn't it be helpful, I thought, to have some background in local Italian cooking and culture before you started out on an expedition like this? Then you would know what to look for, and, if not, you could at least ask the right questions.

The idea didn't really take shape until a couple of summers later, when a fellow journalist, Anne Roberts, and I were looking for a new project. We were walking around our east end neighborhood, and as we passed a playground of Chinese and Indian kids, it suddenly struck us what a cosmopolitan city Vancouver had become. We have a well-developed cultural diversity here that rivals the mountains and the beaches as an attraction for tourists and residents alike. Why not a guidebook to all of this? The lightbulb went on, and the book was born, title and all.

We decided to limit ourselves to the ethnic neighborhoods that had a geographic center—Chinatown, Japantown, Greektown, Little India, and Little Italy. From the beginning, we knew that the book could never be comprehensive—we couldn't possibly include every Chinese vegetable or all the saree shops in Little India—but we also wanted to do a lot more than compile lists of names and addresses. We wanted *Ethnic Vancouver* to be an explorers' book that would take you inside these communities—tell you how to find your way about, tip you off to the best shops and restaurants, and introduce you to the local people.

Unfortunately, other commitments, particularly the birth of her daughter, Kate, meant that Anne Roberts couldn't complete this book with me. But she has continued to be a guiding spirit.

I'd also like to thank the very special people who took me shopping, walking, and eating in their neighborhoods: Bev Nann, Betsy Johnson, Koko, Mitchiko Sakata, Dick Woodsworth, Maud Dias, Peter Patel, Sophie and Chris Dikeakos, Andromaque Vatsis, Donatella Geller, and Enzo Gueraria. Along the way I received help from so many others, including Rani and Batu Dutt, Tom Graff, Ram and Nimo Hira, Karen Lee, Ritta Katajamaki, Candace Kerr, Ray McAllister, Gillian McNair, Dave Murdoch, Mrs. Vassiliki Pasaklidis, Daljit Singh Sandhu, Margaret Stott, Joe Wai, Hayne Wai, and Tameo Wakayama. And special thanks to Leonard Angel who always gives me good advice.

The day I met illustrator Barb Wood was a lucky one for me and for anyone who comes to own this book. From the first, she fell in love with the project and throughout has given her all and a lot more. (Her drawings make *Ethnic Vancouver* not just a guidebook but a gift book as well.) My publisher, David Hancock, was enthusiatic about this book from the very moment he read the proposal, and throughout my editor, Kelly Allen, has shown unerring good judgement.

A note on spelling: although I have chosen the most common spellings, you might well find variations on different menus and package labels as only one of the languages, Italian, comes from Roman script.

Finally, as with any neighborhood, stores and restaurants do come and go, and probably by the time you're reading this book, some wonderful new shop will have opened or another changed hands or gone out of business. In most cases the places mentioned in this book have been around for several years, but if you're making plans to eat out, it might be wise to phone ahead first. Otherwise, enjoy.

Nitobe Gardens (U.B.C.)

Tatami dining room

JAPANTOWN

Japanese restaurants are opening all over Vancouver and there is a new and growing western appreciation for the Japanese food and culture of those tiny islands across the Pacific. It's a perfect time to get out and explore Japanese Vancouver.

You can start with old Japantown. The heart is Oppenheimer Park, between Dunlevy and Jackson streets, facing north onto Powell, the main shopping street. In the old days the park was the focal point for the Japanese community, especially on Saturdays when the Asahi Baseball League held some of the best games in town. In 1942 the entire community was evacuated to internment camps in the interior, and after the war was over very few came back to live here. However, in the last ten years there has been a lot of new retail activity, and on a busy weekend the grocery and fish shops here are humming. There's more shopping and eating just around the corner on East Hastings street.

Downtown at Robson and Thurlow there's a relatively new group of restaurants, piano bars, fast food shops, and gift stores, which have grown up in the last few years to serve the growing Japanese business community and the huge Japanese tourist trade.

Across the Burrard Bridge on 4th Avenue, you'll find a cluster of small shops that sell shoji screens and tatami mats, elegant lacquerware, antique kimonos, and fine porcelain. If you continue out to the University of British Columbia, you'll find the Nitobe Gardens and the new Asian Studies Centre.

Don't forget Steveston. Located at the mouth of the Fraser River, this old Japanese fishing village is one of the most charming spots in the Lower Mainland. On Saturday and Sunday mornings, you can buy fresh fish right off the boats.

Historic Japantown

To remember the old days, when the Powell Street Japanese

community was thriving, half shut your eyes for a moment. It's the twenties or the thirties. **Maikawa Shoten** (you can still see the sign if you look up) at 365 Powell Street was the largest grocery store in the area. Next door Maikawa's son had a fish store, and beside it was one of the bathhouses. There was another across the street, just in from the shoeshine and Nakamura's florist shop, where the Sunshine market is now. A little bit further along the same side of the street was a popular gambling club. This whole stretch of Powell, from Jackson to Main, was once packed with Japanese businesses. Doctors, dentists, banks, and tofu manufacturers—you could find everything on Powell Street.

There was a huge open air fish and vegetable market along Powell street. Every morning as soon as it was light, the local merchants would wash down the sidewalks and Powell was the cleanest street in town. By one old woman's account there were twenty-four Japanese restaurants in the area. In many of them young Japanese girls imitated the geishas of Tokyo and played the shamisen and sang songs to the customers.

Many of the local residents were single men who didn't have proper washing facilities, and a lot of the homes in the area didn't have running water. So from three o'clock until maybe eleven at night, people would come from all over the neighborhood to the bathhouses. Admission was fifteen cents and included soap, a towel, and a straight razor for the men.

Most of the kids went to Strathcona School at Keefer and Princess, but after regular classes, it was down to the Japanese language school for two more hours. In 1928 the community built a new hall for the school at 475 Alexander Street. (You can still see the date written in tile work above the door). This is the only building that is still used for its original purpose.

Alexander and Cordova were the residential streets, from the one hundred block east for about seven blocks, until they both joined Powell. You can still drive along Cordova and see many of the original houses.

Japanese Food

Japanese food is beautiful. It is an elegant and highly refined cuisine in which the apearance of the food is almost as important as the flavor. An ingredient is valued for its taste, freshness, and aesthetic appeal; foods are rarely mixed. Bowls and plates are chosen for the way they harmonize visually with the food—a complex judgement, which takes into consideration religion, history, tradition, and a feeling of unity with nature. There are no heavy sauces or long cooking processes in Japanese food preparation, and only a few major seasonings are used. Japanese food is also low in fats and carbohydrates and high in protein.

Japan is a group of islands surrounded by water, and the sea is naturally a major source of food. Fish of all kinds, from salmon to sea urchin, are eaten both raw and cooked. Seaweed is another dietary staple, along with rice, noodles, and soybean products.

How to Read a Japanese Menu

A Japanese meal can range from a bowl of noodles and green tea to a formal *kaiseki* dinner, which takes three hours to finish. Or you can pick and choose yourself—perhaps some soup, *sashimi* (raw fish), and one of the grilled or deep-fried dishes.

Japanese menus can be a bit overwhelming, even though they all have English translations, so here's a brief guide to the types of dishes that you will encounter.

Sushi literally means "vinegared rice." Regular short-grain rice is washed, boiled in a little less water than usual, and then seasoned with vinegar and hand-cooled. This sushi rice is a little harder and chewier than plain-style rice.

The several types of sushi are easy to identify. For *nigiri-zushi* (the "s" changes to "z" when it's hyphenated) the rice is molded into a flattened egg shape, smeared with a little hot Japanese-style horseradish called *wasabi*, and then topped with a slice of raw fish. The mild flavor of shrimp or red snapper is good to start with. After a bite of pickled ginger to freshen your palate, you can move on to octopus, squid, or sea urchin.

Maki-zushi is sushi-rice, which is rolled around a filling and wrapped in *nori* (seaweed). There are many different kinds of fillings, such as *tekka-maki* (cucumber) and *kampyo* (dried gourd strips). When three or more fillings are combined, you have thicker *futo-maki*. Maki-

13

SOME SUSHI

Nori-Maki Sushi With fish or vegetable fillings, these are good starters. Also oshino-maki (yellow pickle) and futo-maki (fat sushi with five fillings).

"kappa maki" (cucumber roll) &
"tekka maki" (tuna roll)

Tamago If you are not ready yet for raw fish, ease yourself into sushi with this miniature omelet on rice.

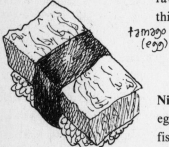

tamago
(egg)

Nigiri-Zushi Flattened ovals of vinegared rice and topped with slices of raw fish, these two are made with shrimp and octopus.

tako
(octopus)

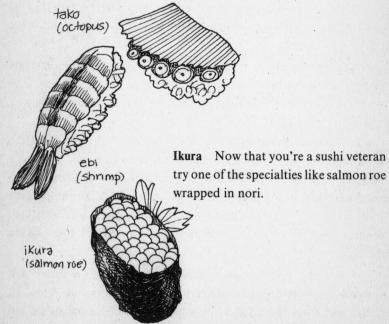

ebi
(shrimp)

Ikura Now that you're a sushi veteran try one of the specialties like salmon roe wrapped in nori.

ikura
(salmon roe)

zushi is made in a long roll, like a fat Havana cigar, and cut into eight pieces. Unless you order a special maki-zushi assortment (which most restaurants have), you'll be served the whole roll, which makes taste testing a little expensive. In some places, maki-zushi is rolled like an ice-cream cone with a variety of fillings and called *te-maki*.

A lot of sushi lovers miss out on *chirashi-zushi,* a bowl of vinegared rice topped with several types of raw fish. When plain boiled rice is topped with chicken and egg or tempura, it's called *donburi*.

Sashimi (sliced raw fish) is a sinful pleasure, and the experience of holding a piece of buttery tuna on your tongue for just moment before it slips down your throat shouldn't be missed. Cutting and serving sashimi is also the chef's finest hour. The filleted fish is usually presented on a small wooden platform in a fanlike arrangement around a nest of shredded *daikon* (Japanese white radish). The bright green dab of paste is wasabi again. Mix it with *shoyu* (soy sauce) and use for dipping.

Sushi or sashimi plus soup is a perfect meal. There are two kinds of soup. Both are based on a standard broth called *dashi*, made from *katsuobashi* (dried bonito fish flakes) and hard, dried *kombu* seaweed. *Suimono* is a clear soup served piping hot in a lidded lacquer bowl. There are usually three garnishes floating in the broth, which add flavor, fragrance, and visual delight to this simple bouillon. Fermented soybean paste is added to make *miso* soup, which is thicker and heartier than suimono. Miso soup is served at every meal, including breakfast.

Japanese salads are small and refreshing. The standard salad in most restaurants is *sunomono*, which means "vinegared things" and may include thin *harusame* noodles, raw or parboiled vegetables, and small pieces of raw or cooked fish. The ingredients are then tossed with a light vinegar dressing. *Aemono* salads have a thicker miso dressing.

Chawan-mushi is a steamed, light, savory egg custard with small pieces of chicken, fish, and vegetable. Most westerners are unfamiliar with this dish, but it makes a good alternative to soup.

Yaki is a good Japanese word to know. It means pan-fried, lightly grilled, or barbecued, as in *yakitori, teriyaki,* and *sukiyaki*. Salmon or chicken teriyaki are good starter dishes if you're a bit shy of Japanese food. The salmon fillet or de-boned chicken is marinated in shoyu, *sake* (rice wine), and *mirin* (sweet cooking wine) for about thirty minutes and then quickly pan-fried. Yakitori are chicken kebabs—small pieces of chicken, green pepper, and onion on bamboo skewers barbecued over

RESTAURANT ETIQUETTE

Japanese etiquette is very complex and ritualistic, and many books are published on the subject. A lot of the rules have fallen upon modern times, but here are some do's and don't's that still stand.

DO   If you are dining tatami style, remove your shoes. In a good restaurant they will be turned toward the exit when you leave, so you can slip into them more comfortably.

DO   Make use of the *oshibori* (hot cloth) brought at the beginning and end of the meal. Japanese put great emphasis on cleanliness, and it's meant for your hands.

DO   Ask if there's a "special" tonight. The menus in Vancouver Japanese restaurants tend to follow a similar pattern, so the special is an opportunity to try something different.

DO   Slurp your noodles. This is not only acceptable but expected. It's also sensible because the cold air you suck in with the food allows you to have it steaming hot.

DO   Try chopsticks. The Japanese variety have pointed ends, which make them a little easier to use than Chinese ones.

DON'T Wave your chopsticks around and use them to point; it's considered rude. And never stick your chopsticks upright in a bowl of rice or use them to take food from someone else's chopsticks. Both these actions are associated with funeral customs and are forbidden at the table.

hot coals. Sukiyaki is another pan-fried dish. Thin slices of beef are quickly sauteed, and then simmered in a sauce with several vegetables.

Mizutaki is a *nabemono* (one-pot) dish. Chicken and vegetables are boiled in a broth, which is usually started in the kitchen and reheated at the table.

Shabu-shabu is often served in a Mongolian hot pot. This is a northern cold weather dish, and Chinese, Japanese, and Russians all use this gleaming round brass pot, which is heated by charcoal. Like mizutaki, the small pieces of food are cooked in the pot and retrieved a few seconds later with chopsticks. Rich shabu-shabu broth is often presented separately as a soup.

With deep-fried Japanese food, the temperature of the oil is crucial and it's always hot enough to fry the food very quickly. You can usually rate a restaurant by checking the *tempura*. If the batter-fried pieces of fish and vegetable are light and lacy, the kitchen standards are probably high. Tempura is a very popular dish, but most restaurants keep to a few standard vegetables and the occasional prawn. Virtually any vegetable and lots of fish can be deep-fried tempura-style.

Katsu (pork) is a lowly meat in Japan but affordable and popular, and more pork items are now appearing in Vancouver restaurants. The most popular is *tonkatsu*—deep-fried breaded pork served with a thick, sharp sauce. These dishes are a bit heavier than normal Japanese restaurant fare.

There are basically three types of noodles served as main dishes. *Udon* and *somen* are white wheat noodles from the north. Udon is fat and somen is thin, and that is the only difference. *Soba* are grey-brown buckwheat noodles from Osaka in the south. They are chewier and tastier than plain wheat noodles. Served cold on a curved lattice-work bamboo tray, they are called *zaru-soba*, a perfect meal for a hot summer day and worth asking for even if they're not listed on the menu. Dip the noodles into the tangy sauce made with wasabi and green onions.

If you like sweets, perhaps you should nip over to Commercial Drive for some fancy ice cream and pastries. Japanese restaurants may have plain sherbet or *yokan* or *an-mitsu* (sweet bean confections) for dessert, but usually the last course is a piece of elaborately cut fruit served with green tea. In a Japanese home a meal would finish with a bowl of plain rice, pickles, and green tea.

sushi bar at the 'aki' restaurant

Barb. Wood.

Tatami Rooms, Sushi Bars, and Noodle Houses

When was the last time you had a private dining room when you went out for dinner? At all but the fast food or noodle places you can have just that at any Japanese restaurant. The rooms are on a raised platform and usually stretch along one side of the restaurant, separated by screens. The floor is covered with tatami straw mats, and what you are experiencing is *tatami* dining. The tables have wells underneath to accommodate westerners not used to sitting Japanese-style on the floor.

Sushi bars are fun and make for good eating. In Japan a sushi bar would be a small counter-style restaurant specializing only in sushi. Here sushi bars are incorporated into larger restaurants, which also have tatami rooms and western-style tables and chairs.

At the polished pine counter you can relax and meditate on the fish of the day presented in the glass cases. Behind the counter is the *itamae* (sushi chef), who has trained for a long time to make a difficult art look simple. Almost every sushi bar has a colored pictograph of the various kinds of sushi so you will know what to ask for.

Noodle houses are new, and welcome, in Vancouver. They are usually open only for lunch, and the basic dish is noodles in broth topped with slices of beef or pork and crunchy vegetables. On a rainy Vancouver day it's a perfect hot, light meal. And you can do it easily for under five dollars per person.

There are several *teppan* or steakhouse restaurants in Vancouver, and, although you can now find them in Japan, they are definitely a recent western invention. These places offer a basic New York steak with a lot of flair. The antics of the chef are fun, but not very authentic.

The Best Restaurants in Japantown

Aki's (374 Powell) is the oldest Japanese restaurant in town. It opened in 1966, and in the early seventies Aki Takeuchi opened the first sushi bar. For a long time, there was a separate menu for Japanese, but recently manager Bob Terakita has added a specialty section to the English menu, with dishes like *Sakana No Nimono*, salmon or red snapper and beancake in a sweet ginger shoyu sauce.

Kamo (363 Powell) is singled out by many Japanese-Canadians for its excellent food and tranquil atmosphere. The lighting is subdued; the tatami decor, simple; and the music, traditional. You can keep it

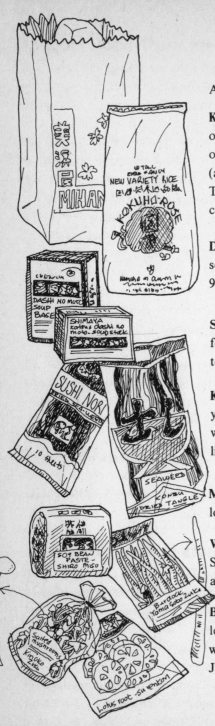

A JAPANESE SHOPPING LIST

Kokuho Rose   The most popular brand of Japanese style short grain rice. In the old days rice was measured in units (about 5 bushels each) and called *kokus*. The worth of a man's land was often counted in potential kokus.

Dashi-No-Moto   Instant dashi broth for soups and seasoning. Add 5 ml (1 tsp) to 900 ml (4 cups) of simmering water.

Sushi-Nori   Paper thin seaweed sheets for making wrapped sushi. Don't forget to lightly toast them before using.

Kombu   Another seaweed for making your own dashi from scratch. Don't wash all the flavor away. Just clean lightly with a damp cloth.

Miso   Available in red, white, or yellow.

Water packed enokitake mushrooms
Salty, long-stemmed mushrooms also available fresh.

Burdock and Lotus Root   Both are pickled vegetables. Cut them up and serve with tea and rice. Only two of dozens of Japanese pickles.

authentic by ordering their special eight-course formal *kaiseki* dinner.

Down the street at 310 Powell the **Fuji** has no tatami rooms or sushi bar. It's a western-style place, popular at lunchtime for local businessmen on the run.

Koji's (347 East Hastings) is the only place in town where you can sit at the sushi bar and watch video cassettes of sumo wrestling. Koji has installed a tempura cook at one end of the sushi bar (in Japan the two would never be mixed), and the experiment has been a success.

If you've got the whole family together, try the **Maneki** across the street (342 East Hastings) where there's a special "panda plate" for children, including rice, noodles, chicken, and chawan-mushi.

The **Edo Ya** (715 East Hastings) has a large central barbecue much like the teppan houses downtown, but this is simpler and more authentic dining.

A Shopping Guide to Japantown

Japantown is divided into two shopping sections. The old section is along the three and four hundred blocks of Powell Street. The newest part of Japantown is a series of restaurants and shops (mostly groceries) strung along East Hastings from the three hundred to the seven hundred block.

Although there is only one gift shop in Japantown, the food stores all stock a good supply of dishes and kitchenware that can make excellent small presents. The imported food products themselves are also tempting as gifts because of the exquisite Japanese style of design and packaging.

Some of the best Japanese gift shopping is found outside Japantown on 4th Avenue. These shops are discussed in a later section.

Food Markets in Japantown

Mihamaya (392-394 Powell) is the oldest food store in the area and stocks everything from comic books to canned soup. Loyal customers claim Mihamaya has the highest turnover and thus the freshest stock in town.

The **Sunrise Market** at 300 Powell is not specifically Japanese, but, for a lot of the old people, it's a favorite spot for fresh vegetables. Sunrise stocks a lot of Japanese foods (as well as Canadian and

Sunrise Market, Powell Street

DAIKON

Boxes of daikon are almost a landmark on Powell Street. Look for a tight skin and a fresh appearance. A withered skin means the root is far too pungent. In Japanese cooking daikon is most commonly grated into long, fine strands and used as a condiment alone or in sauces. Grated daikon will keep three to four hours covered in the fridge.

When pickled, daikon turns bright yellow and changes its name to takuan.

Chinese), and the prices are very good.

Shimizu Shoten (349 East Hastings) is the largest Japanese food store in Vancouver. You can find everything from the latest pop songs and current magazines to Shiseido cosmetics. Shimizu also sells in-house packaged sushi as well as Japanese tea confections called *manju*— small, round steamed cakes in pastel colors, filled with sweet *azuki* (red bean paste).

Don't miss Shimizu's excellent selection of dishes, particularly the stacked lacquered boxes. At New Year's each box contains a special cold dish of shrimp, chicken, or assorted sushi. The boxes also appear at picnics (a perfect combination of practicality and beauty), and a Japanese friend of mine uses two for a lunchbox—one filled with cooked beef or chicken, the other with rice and pickles.

Mikado (701 East Hastings) also has a good selection of tableware from Japan and gets high points for its low prices. **T. Amano** (1139 East Hastings) makes his own tofu on the premises as well as carrying the usual selection of imported foodstuffs.

Shoyu to Shiitake: A Shelf-by-Shelf Guide to a Japanese Food Store

A Japanese grocery can be confusing. Everything seems to be wrapped in plastic, and it all looks the same. In fact, imported foods must be labeled in English, so every Japanese product does have a clearly printed white label pasted on the package, giving the ingredients in English. This certainly helps, but you still might not know what to do with it, or when. So here's a brief guide to a Japanese food store.

A few things are easy to recognize. Japanese-style rice is short grain, and, though it's usually sold in 11-kilogram (25-pound) bags, small plastic 900-gram (2-pound) bags are now available. The most common brand, Kokuho Rose, is packed in the United States.

Japanese rice should be washed three or four times and allowed to stand about half an hour before cooking. Use a heavy-lidded pot and 300 ml (1 1/5 cups) of water for each 250 ml (1 cup) of rice. Bring to a rolling boil and simmer for twenty minutes. Leave the rice to stand, covered, fifteen to twenty minutes before serving.

If you're looking for katsuobushi for soup stock, you'll find it in large bags or boxes. Kombu is another essential ingredient for stock and

matsutake mushrooms

enokitake mushrooms

shiitake mushrooms

burdock (gobo)

lotus root (renkon)

COMMON AND UNCOMMON JAPANESE MUSHROOMS

Matsutake Mushrooms Japanese truffles can cost fifty dollars each. They grow naturally in the Lower Mainland, and many Japanese-Canadians take holidays in the fall to hunt for matsutake. The caches are top secret, and you'll have to find your own.

Enokitake Mushrooms Buff-colored and sold in clumps, these tiny fungi are crisp and mild flavored.

Shiitake Mushrooms Yellowish brown with velvety caps, shiitake are best when the cap edges curl under.

Shiitake are now cultivated in the lower mainland, so fresh ones are often available.

Soak dried shiitake in water for about one-half hour and cut off the tough stems.

JAPANESE FRESH VEGETABLES

Gobo A light brown root often sold in sticks without a top or tail. Test for firmness and soft spots, and store in plastic in the refrigerator.

Renkon Don't worry about size. Look for firmness and light, even color. Avoid large blemishes.

comes in large, flat, dark brown sheets. But there are also many varieties of instant dashi called *dashi-no-moto*, sold in small jello-sized boxes or single packets. As all brands seem to be acceptable, you can choose by price or by the package design you like best.

Often a whole aisle will be given over to rice crackers. The choice of shape and size is overwhelming, and you can spend anywhere from sixty cents to over twenty dollars. The crackers are made of rice flour and flavorings—you can often see little greenish black flecks of seaweed, which give the crackers a salty edge that goes well with beer. With a few variations, most taste more or less the same.

You'll see lots and lots of noodles; there are dried ones on the shelves and water-packed fresh or cooked ones in the cooler. To cook fresh and dried noodles, add to boiling water. As the water comes back to a rolling boil add 250 ml (1 cup) of cold water. Do this several times until the noodles have cooked through. Just drop precooked noodles in boiling water for a few minutes until they are heated.

There will be at least one large cooler jammed with sealed plastic packages of colored vegetables—strips and tidbits of bright green, red, yellow, hot pink, and deep purple. They're all pickles. The Japanese love pickles and serve them at every meal. Virtually anything can be pickled. The most popular is *takuuan* (pickled white radish). It's sold whole and can be up to 30 centimeters (1 foot) long. Try pickled cucumber or eggplant. Cut them to the size you like and serve with rice or as a regular condiment.

In the cooler you'll also find soybean products like *tofu*, made from the pressed curds of soybean milk. Cut into pieces for noodle toppings, soup garnishes, and additions to one-pot dishes. You'll also find red, yellow, and white miso. Savory red miso is most popular for soups (just dissolve one spoonful in 250 ml [1 cup] of dashi).

To complete your Japanese meal you must have *cha* (green tea). The grades are not always clearly labeled, and price alone doesn't guarantee quality. So ask for *bancha*, if you want everyday tea, *sencha* for guests, and *gyokuro* for very special occasions. Powdered tea, called *matcha* or *hiki-cha*, is reserved exclusively for the tea ceremony. *Genmai-cha* is another type of bancha and is easy to identify by the little round brown grains of roasted rice mixed in with the tea leaves. The nutty flavor of genmai-cha is very popular.

There are only a few fresh vegetables in a Japanese food store.

CHAWAN MUSHI

This steamed savory egg custard is a favorite Japanese dish that Westerners have been slow to pick up on. Special lidded chawan mushi dishes are inexpensive and give an authentic touch. As an alternative, use custard cups or even tea mugs covered with foil.

You will need: 500 ml (2 cups) dashi (homemade or instant) at room temperature

3 eggs

Soy sauce

Salt

4 pieces uncooked chicken

4 raw shrimp

A handful of dried or fresh shiitake mushrooms (soak dried shiitake in water until soft)

A handful of snow peas

A handful of watercress

Put a piece of chicken, one shrimp, and one quarter of the mushrooms, snow peas, and watercress into each chawan mushi cup.

Flavor dashi with salt, soya, and mirin to taste (about 5 ml (1 tsp) of each.

Beat eggs into flavored dashi, and whisk until foamy.

Pour egg mixture over the ingredients in each cup.

Place the cups in a covered steamer (or large stovetop pot with about 2 centimeters of water) for about ten minutes or until custard is formed. If liquid is clear, the chawan mushi is done.

Keep the lid on, and serve hot.

Daikon is everywhere. This giant white radish comes in a variety of shapes and is usually grated and served as a condiment or mixed into a dipping sauce. Daikon is supposed to be good for the digestion. *Gobo* (burdock) is a Japanese favorite valued for its energy-giving properties. The thick potato skin should be well scrubbed and soaked in cold water to remove the bitter flavor. Its mild flavor makes it good for simmered dishes and tempura.

You might have to go to Chinatown to find *renkon* (lotus root). It's an aquatic plant found in all the Asian cuisines. From the outside, this sausagelike vegetable isn't very appealing, but the long hollows running through each link make it quite stunning when cut into rounds. Light and crunchy, it's another good tempura vegetable.

The English call it savoy cabbage. Chinese call it sui choi. In Japanese it's called *hakusai*. The long, thin leaves are pale green in color, and you can cut the whole head crosswise for sukiyaki and the other nabemono dishes.

There are three varieties of Japanese mushrooms. Everyday fresh or dried *shiitake*; long, graceful button-topped *enokitake* mushrooms, usually found water-packed in the cooler; and the rare *misutake* mushroom. The latter pine-flavored fungi are so hard to find, they are literally worth their weight in gold.

Fish

Although **Fujiya** (423 Powell) carries a good stock of imported foodstuffs, the specialty here is fresh fish, and the store is dominated by a large delicatessen-style counter where you can choose from prepared abalone, octopus, squid, smelts, perch, and, the favorite, tuna.

The owner, Mr. Shig Hirai, or any of the store employees are most helpful with information about how to serve any of their fish. They will also undoubtedly encourage you to try their ready-made onion, potato, and gobo tempuras. Mr. Hirai is a creative and aggressive businessman, and his tempura, breaded fish balls, and fish cakes are beginning to turn up in different spots all over the city. You'll recognize his little packages of sushi at Granville Island Market. They come from the back of the store where there is a small take-out sushi counter.

Kay's Seafood (338 Powell) has been serving local shoppers for many years. Kay's customers are loyal and like his whole fish that they

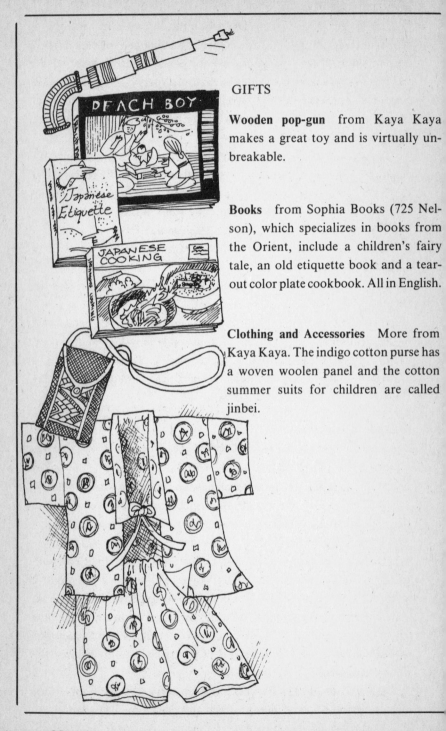

GIFTS

Wooden pop-gun from Kaya Kaya makes a great toy and is virtually unbreakable.

Books from Sophia Books (725 Nelson), which specializes in books from the Orient, include a children's fairy tale, an old etiquette book and a tear-out color plate cookbook. All in English.

Clothing and Accessories More from Kaya Kaya. The indigo cotton purse has a woven woolen panel and the cotton summer suits for children are called jinbei.

can clean and prepare themselves. Kay's is also famous for its *surimi* (ground white fish) for fish balls and its homemade fish cakes, some of which are mounted on small pieces of pine. These Kakuoboko cakes are retailed through many other Japanese stores.

Gift Shopping

Evergreen Enterprises (390 Powell) has been around for more than twenty years, and the selection of rice papers has always attracted Vancouver art students. The plain, colored sheets are still in the two-dollar range, but hand-printed paper is getting expensive to import and retails over ten dollars. The owner, Mrs. Kyoko Sumi, is a gracious woman who always takes time with her customers. She spent half an hour showing me how to make a rice paper lantern, though, in the end, the patterned sheet was so dramatic I just pinned it to the wall above my desk. Mrs. Sumi and her daughter also make short kimono coats and sell the work of local Japanese-Canadian potters.

Robson and Thurlow: More Restaurants

It's too early to call this area Japantown II, but there's an amazingly high concentration of Japanese eating places within a few blocks of this major downtown intersection. These are some of the best.

Kamei Sushi (811 Thurlow) is a Canadian branch of a very successful chain of restaurants in Japan. The atmosphere is bright and lively; the menu simple, easy to read, and planned with an eye to western taste. Understandably, there are lineups every night.

Judging by the lunchtime lineups, the **Minoya Japanese Delicatessan** at 1051 Robson has hundreds of downtown fans. The food can be greasy, but it's cheap and plentiful. Choose from one of the five combination plates (you can't spend much over three dollars here), or order yakitori or assorted sushi a la carte. They'll wrap your styrofoam plate for take out, or you can eat standing at the wooden bar. Minoya also has a small grocery selection as well as dishes and lacquerware.

One of the newest restaurants is the **Kisshin** (1536 Robson). It has an open kitchen behind the sushi bar and a menu that includes beef sashimi as well as daily specials. The Kisshin also offers three kinds of formal *kaiseki* dinners planned exclusively for you by the chef. Reservations must be made a week in advance.

'kaya kaya' at 2037 west 4th avenue

BARB·WOOD.

The **Sapporo Ramen** (518 Hornby) is an authentic Japanese noodle house. Open only until early evening, it's mainly a lunch place. Although the decor is simple, it still manages to create an air of Japanese elegance. Try their *yakisoba* (beef and vegetables on fried noodles) or one of the rice dishes like *oyako don* (chicken and vegetables with egg on rice).

Fourth Avenue: Gift Shopping and Other Treats

From downtown it's a fast trip across the Burrard Bridge to 4th Avenue. You could spend a whole day at **MG 5** (1946 West 4th) soaking in the Japanese baths and having your hands manicured, toes pedicured, hair washed and cut, and, for the men, a nice close shave. The highlight is the massage. *Shiatsu* massage locates the body's pressure points and releases energy trapped in the muscles. After an hour's workover, which includes someone walking down your back, you will be floating on air.

Futons to Sleep On (2173 West 4th) carries locally made *futons* (sleeping mats) that are one hundred percent cotton and make a dandy roll-up bed. The shop also sells futon frames, tatami mats, and *shoji* rice paper screens. At present the owners are battling federal government regulations requiring all mattresses to be treated with a boric acid fire retardant. The futon people want to keep their product completely natural.

Kaya Kaya at 2037 West 4th is a special store. The owner, Mitchiko Sakata, came to Vancouver a dozen years ago and, since then, has been one of the moving forces in the Japanese-Canadian community. She also has exquisite taste, and her shop is filled with a fascinating selection of textile products (including clothes), lacquerware, rice paper stationery, and fine bamboo baskets and trays.

One of the specialties at Kaya Kaya is *Imari-Arita* china. Named after the district in southern Japan where production of this fine porcelain began in the 1600s, early Imari was blue and white (the glazes came from China) but soon developed its distinctive red and gold patterns. These contemporary pieces are expensive, but you won't find a better selection anywhere else in Vancouver.

Your kids will love Kaya Kaya. They'll find wooden yo-yos, noisemakers, and tops, and let them test their skills on *daruma otoshi*. This little man is made from a stack of freestanding colored blocks, and

Antique dolls at 'Kimono Ya'

A SELECTION OF DOLLS FROM KIMONO-YA

These figurines are displayed on a step-chest, a multi-use piece of furniture often found in a merchant's house. The side drawers and cupboards were used for storage, the steps were just that, a stairway to join one floor with another.

The boxed dolls are play dolls for little girls; they're about fifty years old. The freestanding clay dolls are antique pieces from Kyoto. Some of them represent gods that bring wealth or happiness to the family.

the trick is to knock out one of the pieces with a tiny hammer and still keep daruma standing.

Kimono-Ya (3600 West 4th) is well worth a special trip. The shop takes its name from owner Makoto Inuzuka's first love, antique kimonos. The stunning robes of painted and embroidered silk can be worn (Makoto will give full instructions), but they also make impressive wall hangings.

Japanese peasants couldn't wear fine silk in the Edo period (1600-1868), so a cotton industry developed. The result was a specially hand-woven indigo dyed cotton with white geometric designs, called *kasuri* or *ikat.* Kimono-Ya has some old hand-woven pieces and like Kaya Kaya also stocks short coats and peasant pants made from contemporary machinemade ikat cloth. The balloon-style pants soften up after washing, and they are wonderfully comfortable.

A word about shoes. The wooden platform style, called *geta*, are for outdoor wear and were originally designed to give the wearer height. Inside they are exchanged for brocade or embroidered *zori*.Both styles are available at Kaya Kaya and Kimono-Ya.

There's also a new sushi bar near the 4th Avenue shopping district that is well worth a detour. **Kibune** (1508 Yew Street) specializes in tofu dishes. Try their deep-fried bean cake with meat sauce or the barbecued tofu steak with miso sauce.

Night Life

Although westerners are crowding into Japanese restaurants, very few people know about the piano bars. At first glance they look like ordinary lounges. The difference is in the entertainment, which is provided by the customers. Each of the bars has an electric organ and a resident young lady musician, but the tunes are up to the patrons. A microphone is left on the bar, and as the night wears on everyone gets up and sings—ballads, folk tunes, and pop tunes—all, of course, in Japanese.

There are two piano bars in Vancouver, and both are associated with restaurants. **Club Joe** (715 East Hastings) has been around for years. It's a small and intimate place, largely frequented by young men. **Kamei-no-tonari** ("next to Kamei") is right beside the Kamei Sushi restaurant (turn left at the top of the stairs). It has a more sophisticated

SAKE

A proper sake set has five cups (*saksuki*) and two small porcelain flasks (*tokkuri*). One tokkuri is used for pouring; the other, for heating the sake.

To heat sake, place the tokkuri in a pan of hot water for several minutes over low heat. There are exact temperatures for heating sake, but the best test is a drink. It needs to be warm because that way the rice fragrance of the sake is released. Sake can be killed by heat and light, however, so it should be stored in a cool, dark place.

As for sake etiquette, don't pour your own. Watch how your companions' sakzukis are doing, and pour for them. They in turn will do the same. Acknowledge their gesture by holding your cup to receive the sake.

When you raise your glass for a toast the word is *kampai*.

uptown style and seats close to one hundred. You can order sake in a piano bar, but beer and scotch are far more common. Ask for a little plate of salted cuttlefish to go with your drinks.

Japanese Culture

Ikebana, bonsai, traditional music, tea ceremony, and martial arts—there are dozens of classes in traditional Japanese arts you are welcome to join. The martial art clubs have their own headquarters, but the others are best contacted through the **Japanese Canadian Citizens Association (JCCA)** office at 475 Alexander Street. Mary Orishi is in the office every Tuesday and Thursday from ten o'clock to two o'clock and can give you the specifics on what's being offered where.

Ikebana is much more than putting flowers in a vase. The basis of ikebana is a moment of spiritual contact with nature. Specific flowers and plants are used in each season, and the various designs use harmony of line to express the changing patterns of the natural world. There are many styles of ikebana, from strict classicism to more individualistic modernism. The Ikebana Association can direct you to the kind of class you might want.

For gardeners, the Bonsai Association offers regular workshops in the art of planting and pruning miniature trees. The club also has a spectacular two-day show every spring at the Japanese Language School. And in March keep an eye out for the Japanese Gardeners Association plant sale at King Edward Mall at 25th and Oak.

Vancouver's master *koto* teacher, Mrs. Miyoko Kobayashi, has just passed on the presidency of the Vancouver Koto Ensemble to her daughter, Mrs. Teresa Marumoto. The koto is a large stringed instrument, which is laid on the floor and played in a sitting position. The Ensemble recently marked its twenty-fifth year of teaching in Vancouver, and non-Japanese are welcome to join the classes.

In conjunction with the opening of the Nitobe Gardens over twenty years ago, a Urasenke Tea Ceremony group was formed here by Mrs. Noriko Watanabe, who studied the art of *chanoyu* (teaism) in Japan for nine years before coming to Vancouver. The present-day tea ceremony is highly ritualized and can last for several hours. Mrs. Watanabe's group accepts new members and still performs the tea ceremony at the Nitobe Gardens and during various Japanese festivals.

35

BEER AND WINE

Japanese Kirin Beer   It's now available at the piano bars and in most liquor stores. Though pricey like all imports, the crisp, fresh taste is worth the extra cost.

Whiskey   It is very popular in Japan and is drunk alone or with food.

It is always taken with water and ice. Otherwise, the strong flavor of the liquor would overpower the delicate tastes of the food.

Suntory whiskey from Japan is available in specialty stores and is a light, mild scotch specially brewed to combine well with Japanese cuisine.

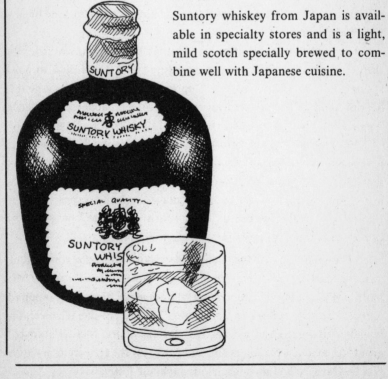

Young boys will probably enjoy *kendo* (fighting with wooden swords). For the best lessons, try the Kendo club at the **Renfrew Community Centre,** run by Mr. Noda. The **Vancouver Judo Club** is at 1133 East Hastings, under the leadership of Mr. T. Tamoto. Karate is a dancelike form of unarmed combat, and the **Vancouver Shito Karate Dojo** is located at 11 West 61st.

The Go Club meets weekly at the Japanese Language School. This intricate board game is played with small black and white stones, and it takes at least thirty hours to understand the basics. After that, players spend a lifetime trying to improve their game and climb the Go hierarchy.

At one time the Japanese used kites for sending secret messages and conveying supplies and food during military campaigns. Today the designing of kites remains a high art, which Dan Kurahashi, a Tokyo kite-maker now living in Vancouver, is trying to promote through his company, Fujin, which buys kites from the top Japanese craftsmen and re-sells them in North America. The prices are steep (several hundred dollars), but the products are one of a kind, like Dan's own train kite, made out of two hundred individual small square kites in a stylistic sparrow design. Contact him through the B.C. Kite Association.

Vancouver now has a full-time Japanese cooking school, called **Yuri's** (243 West 8th). Lily Matsushita's courses also include an introduction to Japanese customs and etiquette.

A word for the *Katari Taiko* (talking drummers). Go out of your way if you have to, but don't miss them. This is primitive, powerful music with lots of drumming and loud chanting. The form has recently been revived in Japan and picked up by Japanese-Americans in San Francisco and San Diego. Several masters have given classes, and Vancouver now has its own group. Katari Taiko perform at most of the local Japanese festivals.

Finally, if you want to learn the Japanese language, there are lots of opportunities in Vancouver. Formal Japanese takes many years, but basic conversation is not too difficult.

Continuing Education at the University of British Columbia regularly offers classes at all levels, and you can keep up your conversational skills between courses at the Asian Centre, where they often have small discussion groups. The Japanese Language School welcomes non-Japanese children. Classes are held every school day

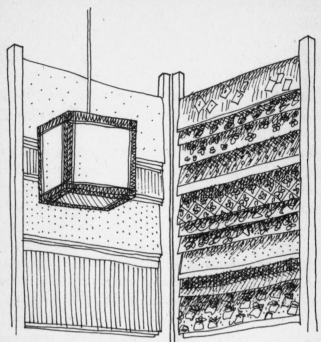

Paper + paper lantern at 'Evergreen'

CHIYOGAMI

Fancy patterned rice paper is called *chiyogami*. It had its origin in 1700 in Kyoto and was made of the best-quality paper.

As it became more available, peasants used chiyogami to make paper dolls, which have now become a fine craft. Mrs. Sumi's paper is often used for that purpose today, and displays of these intricate tiny figures can be seen at the Japanese festival.

afternoon and on Saturday mornings.

Festivals and Holidays

The most important Japanese celebration is unfortunately the least public. New Year's festivities can go on for seven days, and most of it happens in private homes where there is a lot of visiting and eating. Preparation usually starts about December 27 with the pounding of the *mochi* rice. Sweet, steamed glutinous rice is placed on a waist-high block of wood with a concave depression carved on the top. Two men with huge mallets pound the rice, while a third adds and takes away rice between each stroke. The rice is pounded until it has a gumlike consistency, and then the women make it into small, round cakes, which are grilled and dipped in shoyu. The tradition of the mochi is that you pound all your sufferings of the past year into one smoothness and then start the new year with a clean surface.

There's usually a mochi pounding that you can watch just before the new year at the Strathcona Community Center. Call 254-9496 for the exact date.

There are two summer festivals held on the Powell Street Grounds. The *Obon* Festival in July is sponsored by the Buddhist Church beside the park on Jackson Street, and is a day for welcoming the spirits of the ancestors. The religious ceremonies are held in the church the day before the public celebrations. On the day itself, the ladies of the church have food booths and there are demonstrations of ikebana, bonsai, judo, and karate.

The annual two-day Powell Street Festival, usually in August, is a purely secular event to bring the scattered Japanese community home to Powell Street and demonstrate that the spirit of the community is still alive. The events are much like the Obon Festival, but on a bigger scale, with food booths from restaurants all over the city.

Around Town

Japanese food is so popular in Vancouver now that you could probably eat in a different place every evening for a month. But there are some standouts worth noting.

Mr. Ito, the chef at the **Kappa Restaurant** (4067 Cambie), gets high

39

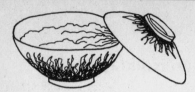

large rice bowl

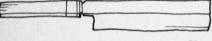

noodle basket

condiment dish

TABLEWARE AND UTENSILS

Rice Bowl Use the large one when you make domburi or chazuki sushi.

Noodle Basket For draining and serving noodles.

Condiment Dish You can put one at each place for pickles and sauces.

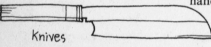

Knives

Vegetable Knives These are the most useful knives in a kitchen. For small quantities, they beat a food processor hands down.

bamboo mat (sudare)

KITCHEN UTENSILS

Sudare It is inexpensive and a must for rolling sushi.

Bamboo Baskets Use them for draining noodles.

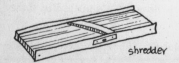

draining baskets

Shredders You'll find many types of shredders or graters in the kitchen section of most Japanese food stores. It's handy to have at least one for getting the right size of long daikon filaments.

shredder

marks from a number of customers, including one of the best Japanese cooks I know. And a faithful clientele has been coming back to the **Jinya** (567 West Broadway) for many years. Tojo, the owner and chef, takes special care of the customers he likes. The Jinya is another restaurant that has daily specials posted.

Koji II is in the new Broadway Plaza complex and has done a roaring business since it opened in February 1981. This is the largest and most dramatic restaurant in town, with a stunning view over False Creek. Koji himself is no longer associated with this place or the one on East Hastings, but the kitchen standards are still high. Try their special maki-zushi about 7 cm (2½ in.) in diameter and filled with barbecued salmon skin, crab cake, cucumber, and Japanese mayonnaise. Fantastic.

Ariston (2828 Granville) has the best silks from Japan and specializes in long *obis*, the sashes for kimonos. Prices can go as high as three hundred dollars.

For a special afternoon, visit the **Nitobe Gardens** at the University of British Columbia. Inside the thatched roof gateway you will find a hundred things to delight you in this authentic Japanese Garden—the stone lanterns symbolizing lighted pathways, the manmade lake filled with golden carp, and the zig-zag Yasu-hasi bridge guiding you through the iris garden. This is truly a place for contemplation, relaxation, and meditation.

While you're at the Nitobe Gardens, don't forget to visit the **Asian Studies Centre.** The Centre functions primarily as a research center for scholars in Oriental Studies, but its mandate also includes making links with the local community. Typical events might include a workshop on modern Japanese business history, films about Japanese-Canadian artists, or a special lecture on architecture by a visiting professor from Japan.

The downstairs area of the Centre has a small display hall with artifacts from Japan, China, and India. The art gallery on the same floor has changing exhibitions, which are open to the public. There's also a library here with a fine collection of books in the original languages, and special borrowing privileges are available for non-students.

The Asian Centre publishes a bulletin every four months to let you know what's going on. To get on the mailing list, call 228-4686.

41

custard

tempura

salad

rice

soup

chopsticks

DISHES

The custard cup is for chawan mushi only—this savory egg custard is steamed in the lidded pot. The soup bowl is deeper than the rice bowl to keep in the heat. Clear soups are served in covered lacquered bowls. The small, square dish is a traditional one for serving salads. Chopsticks rest on a small holder.

Out of Town: A Trip to Steveston

The best time to visit Steveston is very early on a Saturday or Sunday morning. As soon as it gets light, the Steveston fish market opens on the government wharf, and, from all over the Fraser River and up the coast, fishermen come to sell straight from their boats.

The heart of Steveston is the three or four blocks of Moncton Street just up from the wharf. To get there, cross the Oak St. Bridge and take Hwy. 99 going south. Go west on the Steveston Hwy. until you reach No. 2 Road. Turn south and continue to Moncton Street. Follow Moncton west until you reach the village. Here's an eclectic mix of businesses with a new South American import shop; a French bookstore, **La Mouette;** a superb Danish Bakery (try their hand-dipped chocolates); and one of the best hardware stores anywhere, **Steveston Marine and Hardware.** The tiny **Steveston Museum** (upstairs from the post office) has a photographic history of early Steveston, a guide to the workings of a cannery, and a few rare pieces of jewelry and household goods brought by the early Japanese settlers.

The three Japanese grocery stores in Steveston are all friendly places to shop. The **Marine Grocery** has a reputation as the best butcher. The **Fraser Mart** is a tiny jampacked store, and you can spend hours searching for what you need through the narrow aisles. At the **Hiro Market** you probably will have to ask for what you want, as most of the goods are kept behind the counter.

The most impressive building in Steveston is the **Dojo**—the martial arts center that opened several years ago. Designed in traditional style, it's open to visitors on Sunday. Steveston is a long way to go for judo or kendo classes, but you can be assured of the best teaching from the best Japanese black belt masters available in British Columbia.

If You Want to Know More

The new weekly Vancouver *Shimpo* newspaper is printed in Japanese, but the Japanese Canadian Citizens Association does publish a small monthly newsletter in English that lists upcoming events. For a subscription, call the JCCA.

Although **Tonari Gumi** (573 East Hastings) is officially a drop-in center for elderly Japanese, it is also one of the best places for finding out what's happening in the Japanese-Canadian community. Tonari Gumi is run by the Japanese Community Volunteers, a group of enthusiastic and committed young people.

There are several books documenting the history of the Japanese in Vancouver. The best account is in the *Politics of Racism* by Ann Gomer Sunarhara published in 1981 by Lorimer and Sons. For a semi-fictional treatment of the evacuation, Joy Kogawa's beautifully lyric *Obesan* published in 1982 by Oberon Press is highly recommended.

It could be a trip out to Steveston, a shopping tour of Powell Street, or an hour of quiet in the Nitobe Gardens. Whatever, there are pockets of Japanese culture all around Vancouver and the Lower Mainland. Why not get out and find some of it this weekend?

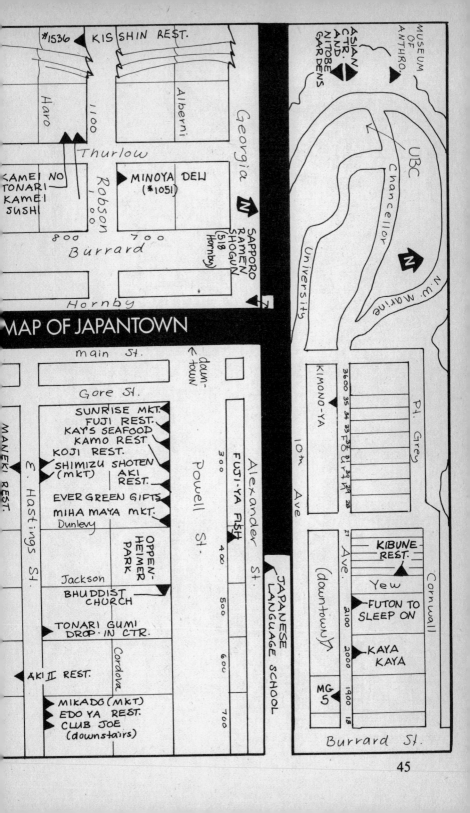

MAP OF JAPANTOWN

Upper left section:

#1536 KIS SHIN REST.

1100

Haro

Alberni

Thurlow

Georgia

Robson
1000

KAMEI NO
TONARI
KAMEI
SUSHI

MINOYA DELI
(#1051)

SAPPORO
RAMEN
SHOGUN
(518
Hornby)

800   700

Burrard

Hornby

Upper right section:

MUSEUM OF ANTHRO.

ASIAN CTR. AND NITOBE GARDENS

UBC

Chancellor

University

N.W. Marine

Lower left section (Japantown):

Main St.

← downtown

Gore St.

SUNRISE MKT.
FUJI REST.
KAY'S SEAFOOD
KAMO REST
KOJI REST.
SHIMIZU SHOTEN (mkt)   AKI REST.
EVER GREEN GIFTS
MIHA MAYA MKT.
Dunlevy

OPPEN-HEIMER PARK

Jackson

BHUDDIST CHURCH

TONARI GUMI DROP·IN CTR.

Cordova

AKI II REST.

MIKADO (MKT)
EDO YA REST.
CLUB JOE
(downstairs)

MANEKI REST.

E. Hastings St.

Powell St.

300

400

500

600

700

FUJI-YA FISH

Alexander St.

JAPANESE LANGUAGE SCHOOL

Lower right section:

KIMONO-YA

3600 35 34 33 32 31 30 29 28

Pt. Grey

10th Ave.

27 Ave.

KIBUNE REST.

Yew

FUTON TO SLEEP ON

(downtown)

2100

2000

KAYA KAYA

MG 5

1900

18

Cornwall

Burrard St.

45

MARKET
681·2618

KWANG·CHOW
Restaurant

NANKING
RESTAURANT

MANDAR
FOOD

BARB·WOOD.

E. Pender Street in Chinatown.

CHINATOWN

The street is humming until late in the evening, the neon lights are bright, and there is always a traffic jam. It's a city within the city, and a part of Vancouver's history. This is Chinatown.

There are over one hundred thousand Chinese-Canadians living in the Lower Mainland, and on the weekends it feels as if they have all come down here to shop, eat, and socialize. When I arrived in Vancouver in the midsixties, Chinatown was largely confined to three or four blocks of Pender Street. But in the last half-dozen years of rapidly increasing immigration—particularly from Taiwan, the People's Republic of China, and Hong Kong—business and retail activity have spilled over to Hastings Street on the north and as far south as Union.

Chinatown is filled with new shops, restaurants, and grocery stores. Ten years ago there was one herbalist shop and an unadvertised bakery in the back of the Hong Kong Cafe; there are at least six of each now. The noodle houses are new, and there are a dozen dim sum places. Chinatown now has Mandarin as well as Cantonese menus, elaborate banquet halls, and fancy night spots. You can buy cosmetics and pop songs from the People's Republic of China, fine gold jewelry, hand-embroidered linens, antique and contemporary artwork, clothes, ceramics, and rattan. Vancouver's Chinatown is an explorer's paradise.

A Historic Walking Tour of Chinatown

The first Chinese came to British Columbia in 1858, heading for the gold fields in Barkerville. A second group of fifteen thousand came as laborers in the 1880s to build the western section of the Canadian Pacific Railway. In both instances, most of the immigration was from the drought-stricken southern province of Kwangtung. The Manchu government, far away in Peking, was politically and economically bankrupt. There was no land and no future for poor rural peasants.

Many came to the new world hoping to make their fortunes. They soon discovered there was no *gum san* (golden mountain) here, but, as hard as life was, it was worse in China.

About fifty feet west of Carrall on the south side of Pender there is a street sign saying *Shanghai Alley*, put up by the city after a freeway fight in the late sixties to acknowledge the historic importance of this part of the city. Though it is nothing now but the back ends of warehouses, Shanghai Alley is where Chinatown began.

After a vicious race riot in 1907, many Chinese lived in a large compound that offered protection from future attacks; its only entrance was on Pender Street. One wing stretched along Shanghai Alley; the other to the west bordered the old rail yards. This huge fortress had seven stories and housed dozens of single men and many families. There were fourteen shops on the ground floor.

Across the street, at 5 West Pender, is the original home of the Chinese Freemasons, a society formed in Canada to support the overthrow of the Manchu government. Leading the fight was Dr. Sun Yat-Sen, now called the father of modern China, who stayed for several months in this building in 1911 while working to raise support from the overseas Chinese in Vancouver.

In 1913, on a seven-thousand-dollar bet that nothing could be done with a six-foot piece of property, Sam Kee constructed what is still the narrowest office building in the world at 8 West Pender. The most recent tenant here is **Kuo Kong Silks**, for many years located at 27 East Pender (you can still see the company name on the tiled entry). Mrs. Sue Gee Jackman sells raw and fine silks by the yard from her tiny shop and is quick to remember the old days when Kuo Kong fitted silk shirts for MacKenzie King. **On Wo Tailors** at 11 West Pender and **Modernize Tailors,** around the corner at 511 Carrall, are among the few custom tailors still left in Chinatown.

Moving east to the unit block where East Pender begins, the *Chinese Times* building is a landmark at the northeast corner. Chinatown's first newspaper has been publishing since 1907. The type is still handset, and the presses run off two editions a day.

The first phase of the **Chinese Cultural Centre** was completed in the fall of 1980 and takes up most of the south side of the block. At one time this was False Creek marshland. In 1905 it was filled in to create the Great Northern Railway Depot. You can still see the "To the Trains"

48

sign on the west wall of the building housing the **Marco Polo Restaurant** (unfortunately slated for demolition at the time of writing).

Behind the train station was the Chungking, one of two Chinatown opera houses. The operas used to come from Hong Kong every fall and winter. These were large, well-appointed theaters with single seats, and the program would run from midmorning till late at night.

The Chinatown Post Office is located in the **Columbia Building** at 103 East Pender. This is one of the oldest buildings in Vancouver, erected just after the great fire of 1886. As you move east along the one hundred block you can see the construction dates noted near the tops of many of the early buildings. The architectural style on this block—with its arches, pillars, and bright colors—is reminiscent of southern China. The inset balconies gave relief from the heat and a chance to watch the business of the street. Some of them contained "cheater stories," which were hidden from the street and from the tax collector, who made his assessment according to floor space.

Most of the buildings in this block were built by Chinese family associations or "tongs," such as the **Wong Society Building** at 23 East Pender (which also housed one of the half-dozen Chinese schools), the Chin Wing Chun Society, and the Mah family building. The tongs were organizations that provided rudimentary social services. New immigrants could always find a place to live, a free meal, and a few dollars to get themselves started. The umbrella **Chinese Benevolent Association** (108 East Pender) set up soup kitchens during the depression, so that the Chinese would not have to accept government relief.

This block also contains some of Chinatown's oldest eating places. **The Ho Ho,** at the southeast corner of Columbia and Pender, hosted early Chinese banquets and, along with the **Ho Inn** (79 East Pender), is still a "greasy spoon" favorite with many who grew up in Chinatown. The **B.C. Royal** at 119 East Pender and the **Hong Kong** at 149 East Pender were the first cafés in Chinatown. Their menus were, and still are, half western and half Chinese.

North of the one hundred block is *Market Alley,* where, in the old days, tiny restaurants used to front for gambling joints. The food had to be good to keep the customers inside on rainy days, and for years the Orange, Green, and Red Doors were the best places to get Chinese food. The **Green Door** is still in business.

Historic Chinatown pretty well stops at Main. The residential

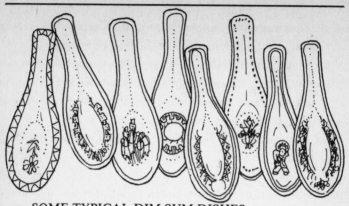

SOME TYPICAL DIM SUM DISHES

Cha Siu Bau   White steamed buns filled with barbecued pork. There are several kinds of *bau* (bun). The chicken filled bun is called gai bau. Min yung bau are sweet and filled with lotus seed paste.

Ha Gau   Minced shrimp is steamed in a transparent won ton wrapper. They are often called shrimp bonnets in English.

Siu Mai   Mixed minced shrimp and pork.

Cheun Fahn   It looks like Italian canneloni. Rolled noodle dough is stuffed with barbecued pork, shrimp, or beef.

Cheun Gyun   You probably call these spring rolls. The same shape as cheun fahn, but this time the pastry is very thin and deep fried.

Pai Gwat   These are little dishes of marinated spare ribs.

Ha Do Si   Shrimp toast.

Lo Mai Gai   A dark green lotus leaf filled with sweet glutinous rice and Chinese sausage, and then steamed.

Ngau Yuk Yuen   Beef meat balls.

Don Tot   The famous egg custard tart. This is sweet, but not too sugary.

When you're finished eating dim sum, the headwaiter will tote up the bill. The price is calculated by adding up the empty plates; each size has a different price. This is perfect eating for the budget conscious.

district **Strathcona** starts at Gore and continues east to Campbell, Hastings and Prior form the north and south boundaries. Some of the houses here were built at the turn of the century for the Vancouver elite, and you can still see some fine examples of Queen Anne gables and lots of ornate gingerbreading. The Chinese began to settle in the area in the thirties, and many still live here. At one point the city government planned to raze the old houses and put in new subsidized developments. The community resisted this so-called "slum clearance," and in 1969 the Strathcona Rehabilitation Programme was introduced to renovate and upgrade existing housing.

An Introduction to Chinese Food

Chinese cooking is geographically divided into four general categories. Since the bulk of immigration continues to be from the area around Canton (Hong Kong is only a few miles away), this southern style of Chinese cooking is the most common in North America.

Cantonese cooking is known for its variety—up to four hundred thousand dishes—and its inventiveness—anything that can be eaten is, from pig's testicles to duck's heads. However, Canton's combination of access to the sea and a mild climate has put most of the emphasis on fresh fish and vegetables, which are kept as close as possible to their natural state by only light stir-frying. The Cantonese are also famous for their soups and tiny steamed dim sum teahouse delights.

While Cantonese seasonings are quite mild, the flavors of northern (also called *Mandarin* or *Peking*) cooking are much stronger. The food is cooked in dark instead of light soy sauce, with lots of garlic and bean paste. Rice is not cultivated in the north, so wheat noodles are the daily staple. Although northerners have a passion for mutton, there is less meat in this diet, and people tend to fill up on steamed buns and dumplings.

Szechuan food from the western province of that name is hot to very hot. The peppercorns can numb your tongue, and get ready for lots of red and green chilis. As in India, these highly spiced dishes are supposed to invigorate the body and counteract the deleterious effects of the humid weather in the western part of China.

From the cosmopolitan seaport of the east comes *Shanghaiese* cuisine. Here the food is cooked a little longer and often preserved in

TIPS FOR EATING IN A CHINESE RESTAURANT

Ignore the decor, unless you want to pay for it. If you're tired or want to talk quietly, the fancier places can be a lot more relaxing.

Order specialties from the region represented by the restaurant—no Peking duck in a Cantonese restaurant!

Don't add soy sauce until you've tasted the food. Otherwise you're making a judgment on the chef's abilities. It's not polite.

Use your soup bowl for rice. Asking for a plate (except at a banquet) is like asking for a fork.

Order Tsingtao Chinese beer if it's available. It's crispy with a bright ginger edge.

There's no dessert (except in northern restaurants). But if you must, the coffee and western pastries at the **B.C. Royal** and the **Hong Kong Café** are excellent.

If there's anything left when you're full, ask for it to be wrapped up and take it home. It's expected that you wouldn't want to waste good food.

wine; drunken chicken is one of the favorite dishes. Salt is also used as a preservative, and fresh fish is a staple of the east coast diet. Soy sauce is mixed with a good deal of sugar, and sweetness is another trademark of eastern cooking.

From Noodle Shops to Banquet Halls: Types of Chinese Restaurants

Chinese like to eat out. A restaurant is a gathering spot during the day and a place to socialize with family and friends in the evening. That is why Chinatown is packed with restaurants for every occasion. And because the cuisine is so highly valued, it is difficult for a bad restaurant—in Chinatown, at least—to survive.

But the variety of restaurants can be confusing. What is a won ton house, and when do you eat there? Can you have dim sum in the evening? How do you plan a Chinese banquet? A visitor will never starve in Chinatown, but to help you get what you want, here is a simple guide to the various types of restaurants.

Most people have had dinner at a Chinese restaurant. You can eat plain at a small place like the **Dai Kee** at 540 Main Street, where the prices are cheap (about five dollars per person), the decor is arborite, and usually there is no liquor license. If your nerves get jangled by the end of the day, you may prefer the relative quiet of one of the larger restaurants like the **Sam Lock** (263 East Pender). If you want really fancy, Chinatown has that too. **The Golden Crown** (108 West Hastings) has carved gold dragons, rich mahogany paneling, crystal chandeliers, and a menu of no less than 250 dishes.

If you want to order on your own, a soup, a vegetable dish, and two or three fish or meat dishes will fill the bill for four or five people. Think about variety when you are ordering, especially in cooking methods. If you're eating Cantonese for example, combine a small hot pot or a deep fried dish with the usual stir-fried style. For a change of pace you can ask the waiter to serve you what a Chinese family might eat.

If you want to try a Chinese banquet, choose one of the bigger restaurants where you already like the food. Give the restaurant a few days notice and clear directions about how much you want to spend per person. For a real feast, plan on twelve to fifteen dollars each and have at least ten people to make it worthwhile.

Dim Sum Service at the W.K. Gardens.

DIM SUM

The **W.K. Gardens** (173 East Pender) is where I was first
introduced to dim sum. Genial owner Wilbert Lim has
been associated with the W.K. since it opened in the early
'30s down the street at 127 East Pender. The original
W.K. Chop Suey seated several hundred and was the first
restaurant in Chinatown to attract western customers
looking for authentic Chinese food. W.K. stands for *wah
kiu* (overseas Chinese).

Many Cantonese restaurants turn into *dim sum* houses at lunchtime. Don't wait for a menu. Just pick what you want from the carts as they're wheeled by. (Dim sum translates as "point to your heart's delight"). The dishes are all small, bite-sized morsels of sweet and savory stuffed dumplings and marinated or braised meats. There are at least 150 dim sum dishes, and it won't be long before you will crave an order of *ha gau* (shrimp dumplings), *pai gwat* (spare ribs), or even *foong jow* (chicken feet).

The noodle or *won ton* houses are a specialty from Hong Kong. This is Cantonese fast food; if you're in a hurry you can be in and out in twenty minutes. The basic dish is stuffed won ton or noodles topped with barbecued duck, pork, or chicken. And do give *congee* a try. This thin rice gruel is one of the favorite Cantonese all-purpose dishes. Flavored with fish, meat, or various other combinations, it is eaten for breakfast, lunch, or a midnight snack.

For a midmorning or late afternoon pick-me-up, try one of the cafés or tea rooms, like the old **Yip Hong Yuen** at the southwest corner of Pender and Gore. The coffee at these places is surprisingly good and is usually the order of the day, although tea is available. For nibbling, order a savory pork bun, a long fried donut, or a couple of delicious *don tots,* the famous Chinese-style egg custard tarts.

The Best Chinese Restaurants

There are dozens of excellent restaurants in Chinatown, and picking the best ones is like choosing between the crown jewels. Here are some of my favorites:

The **Lung Kee** (281 East Pender) is a tiny place that specializes in *Hakka*-style southern cooking, which emphasizes fresh seafood. The prices of the fresh fish swimming in the tank just inside the door can be high, but it's usually worth the difference. The **Janus** on the fringes of Chinatown (236 East Georgia), had a previous incarnation as a Spanish restaurant. Despite the Mediterranean decor, the food is authentic Chinese. Ask for the *Swatow* specialties, which are a little hotter and spicier than the everyday Cantonese dishes.

Every Chinese person I have asked about restaurants always puts **Ming's** (147 East Pender) near the top of his list, especially for elaborate banquets. Later in the evenings the large upstairs dining room turns into

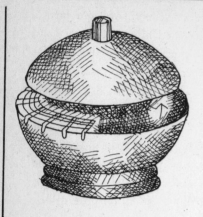

COOKWARE

Wok The metal collar lets you rest the wok on a solid base for cooking over an electric element or gas flame. The side rack is for holding food that has already been cooked.

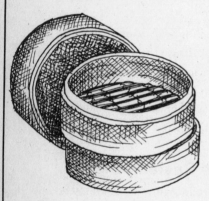

Bamboo Steamers Use one or stack as many as you need for steaming vegetables or dim sum dishes.

Clay pot Bound with thin wire, it's for oven-cooked casserole-type dishes. It also makes an attractive serving dish.

a nightclub. Entertainment is provided by singing stars from Hong Kong, Taiwan, and sometimes Korea.

The dim sum menu at Ming's is excellent, but my first choice is the **First Dim Sum House** (252 East Pender), virtually undiscovered by westerners. Look for the little shrine on the back wall with its offerings of fruit and rice and for the owner of Wah Chun Tong, who comes through with the latest editions of the Chinese newspapers.

The **Daisy Garden Noodle House** (126 East Pender), has the best barbecued duck in town, but for something really different, try the **Great Shanghai** (648 Main), for eastern-style fried noodles and thick congee. Their soybean milk is sweet and savory at the same time and thick enough to eat with a spoon.

For snacks, try the sweet red bean paste buns at the **B.C. Royal Café** (119 East Pender). Their thick, rich coffee also makes this spot worth a special visit.

A Shopping Tour of Chinatown

There are several distinct shopping areas in Chinatown. Pender, west of Main is often identified as the "tourist" section because most of the gift shops are located here, although some of the best jewelry and clothing can be found in the new shops that are springing up along Main Street.

The two hundred block Pender is the main market area with grocery stores, butchers, and fishmongers. These shops also extend north along Gore, and, as the community grows, more and more food stores are opening on East Hastings.

The north side of Keefer is bakery row. For a long time this block was filled mostly with warehouses. There is still one main depot in the middle of the block. Buying and selling starts there in the early morning hours, and, if you can get yourself up, it's a fascinating scene to watch.

The Best Food Stores

Most Chinese shoppers find one store they like and keep to it. Part of this loyalty is a business mutual aid; "I patronize your grocery store, you come to my restaurant or jewelry shop or whatever." For non-Chinese going to shop regularly in Chinatown, this is probably a good idea too, as the store people will quickly get to know you. However,

CHINESE VEGETABLES

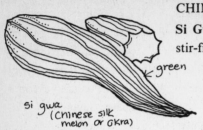

Si Gwa Pare off the ribs, slice, and stir-fry until translucent.

green

si gwa
(Chinese silk
melon or okra)

Dung Gwa Buy by the piece, pare, and cut in small cubes. Boil in soup with pork and dried mushrooms.

white

dung gwa (winter melon)

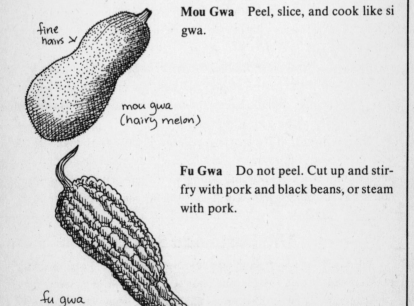

Mou Gwa Peel, slice, and cook like si gwa.

fine hairs

mou gwa
(hairy melon)

Fu Gwa Do not peel. Cut up and stir-fry with pork and black beans, or steam with pork.

fu gwa
(bitter melon)

prices do vary between the stores, so it's often wise to check out a couple of places if you know what you want.

Yuen Fong at 242 East Pender is the biggest of the Chinatown markets. It has a large kitchenware section at the back as well as several aisles of china, cookbooks, and ornamental vases. There's even a small glass case of intricately carved snuff bottles.

The selection of teas at Yuen Fong is outstanding. The marvelous packaging—brightly colored tins, elegant bamboo boxes, and smooth porcelain pots—makes them excellent for gifts, and the prices will also be a pleasant surprise.

Leiku, (262 East Pender) is smaller but jammed to the ceiling with an inventory of over thirty thousand items. If you are a bargain hunter, this store gives a ten percent discount on every sales slip the first Thursday of the month.

Yuen Fong and Leiku are the two big stores on the market block, but there are lots of other little markets with their own specialties and competitive prices. **Wing Hing** (280 East Pender) has its own butcher shop, and **Kowloon Trading** (236 East Pender) has excellent fresh vegetables, and for fresh fruit, try **Man Cheong** (250 East Pender). You'll also like the open-air style of the grocery shops on Gore. Give yourself lots of time to visit several stores.

A Shelf-By-Shelf Guide to a Chinese Food Store

A Chinese food store can be intimidating. Although packages are supposed to have English labels, the translations are often enigmatic. Many of the clerks speak Chinese only, and, because the shops are always busy, it can be hard to find assistance. So for first-timers, let this book be your guide through a typical Chinese market.

The fresh vegetables displayed outside most stores are usually identified only by Chinese characters. Aside from spinach and snow peas, most of them will be unfamiliar. The things that look like melons, squash, or cucumbers are different types of *gwa*. They are sliced up and boiled in soups or used in stir-fry dishes.

There is a large and confusing group of leafy green vegetables called *choy* (cabbage) of which *bok choy* is the most common. *Gai choy* has a similar shape but with thicker dark green stems. Sometimes called

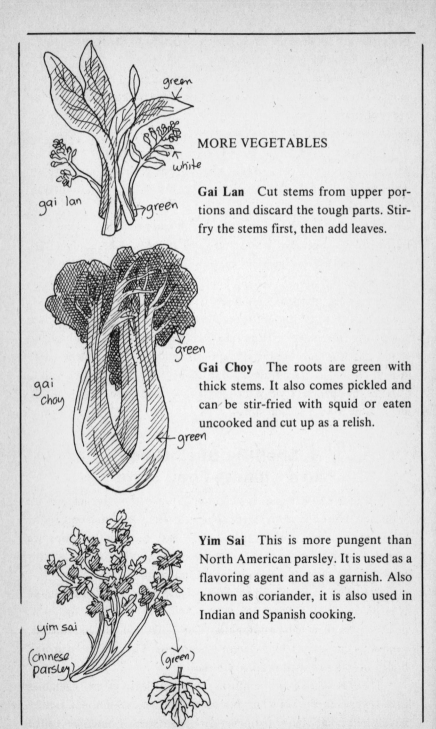

MORE VEGETABLES

Gai Lan   Cut stems from upper portions and discard the tough parts. Stir-fry the stems first, then add leaves.

Gai Choy   The roots are green with thick stems. It also comes pickled and can be stir-fried with squid or eaten uncooked and cut up as a relish.

Yim Sai   This is more pungent than North American parsley. It is used as a flavoring agent and as a garnish. Also known as coriander, it is also used in Indian and Spanish cooking.

mustard greens, gai choy is also used in soup and stir-fry dishes. *Sui choy* is pale yellow; the slim leaves are closely packed like an elongated iceberg lettuce. Slice crosswise, stir-fry quickly, and then add a little water and cook until soft. *Yim sai* is Chinese-style parsely. *Gai lan* is like North American broccoli and is one of the tastiest of the Chinese greens.

Wu tau (taro) is a delicious root-type vegetable. It is usually steamed, mashed, and made into fritters or turnovers. Japanese daikon is another root vegetable and in Chinatown is called *lo bok*. A little lo bok sub-group includes *cheng lo bok* (dark green lo bok) and *hung lo bok* (carrots).

When the weather gets warm, splurge on fresh lichees. Inside the wrinkled wooden shell, the fruit is baby smooth and lightly scented. Yellow Chinese snow pears are juicy and crisp, like apples, and your kids will probably like to suck on pieces of sugar cane. Don't pass by the oranges without a second look. The Chinese take oranges as gifts when they go calling, and insist on the best quality.

Right inside the front door you'll usually find several large ceramic pots of preserved duck eggs, which look like they've been rolled in black or brown sawdust. The brown ones are the famous one-hundred-year-old eggs, a lovely piece of poetic exaggeration. They are coated with lime, salt, ashes, and tea, and are cured for one hundred days. The inside is black and gelatinous with a strong cheesy, almost sulfurous flavor. Just slice and eat as is.

The black eggs are salted and, after cleaning, must be cooked before eating, either boiled whole or broken and steamed. Neither type of duck egg is very expensive, so they are at least worth an experiment. And watch for the pots to empty. The stores often sell them for less than twenty dollars, and they make excellent planters.

Next stop are the large coolers, where you will find won ton skins, *cheun gun* (spring roll wrappers), mandarin bread, and red bean paste buns. The Double Happiness fresh noodles are made locally, and you can buy them direct from the factory at 427 Powell. The freezer has lots of unusual frozen fish like yellow croaker, mudfish, and supmouth.

The jars and bottles section has the basic sauces like soy, oyster, and hoisin. Hot pepper or bean relish, pickled garlic, and sweet vinegary ginger can all be used as condiments, dips for cooked vegetables (raw vegetables don't belong in the Chinese diet), or sliced and served cold as an appetizer or snack.

ma tie
(water
chesnuts)

white

(peeled)

brown

Ma Tie These bulbs grow in shallow, muddy water. Peel and eat fresh or stir-fry with meat or poultry.

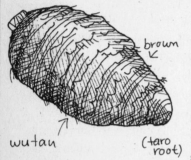

brown

wutau

(taro root)

Wu Tau Peel, slice, and steam until soft. Mash and mix with wheat starch dough, barbecued pork, shrimp, green onions, soy sauce, and seasonings. Form into small pancakes and deep fry for sweet taro fritters.

'green' lo-bak

Lo Bok Peeled, cubed and included with pork in soup, green lo bok is good for the complexion. It's also excellent for cold sores.

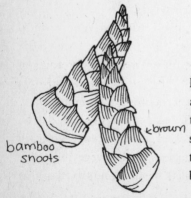

bamboo shoots

brown

Bamboo Shoots A great delicacy when available fresh in the spring. Remove the sheath and cut the tender core into small-sized pieces, and boil in water twenty to thirty minutes. If it is still bitter, boil again in fresh water.

There are usually several shelves of dried and preserved foods packaged in crinkly see-through cellophane bags. The dried greens are a leftover from the days when vegetables were not available in the winter. Most of the soup mixes are for medicinal purposes. Bean curd sticks are popular for vegetarian dishes and sweet soups. The pieces of salted fish are cut up and steamed on little plates, placed over rice while steaming, and then served with fresh ginger and oil. Dried shrimp comes in several different grades as do the meaty dried black mushrooms. If you're going to invest in these expensive fungi, look for fat, unbroken ones. Shark fins for soup are another luxury item, starting at about twenty dollars for a medium-sized packet.

Some of the foods from the People's Republic of China, like sweet vinegar, which is used in making a special childbirth broth for new mothers, or crisp and salty preserved vegetables, are packed in small individual glazed pots. The prices, crock and all, are very low (often less than two dollars), and the colors and designs make them well worth collecting.

Nuts, beans, and rice are usually nearby. The raw peanuts from Chinatown are a real treat when they are deep-fried. Black beans are used in the most popular fish sauces, and red ones are cooked with sugar and used in making pastry fillings. A Chinese friend suggested that sweet glutinous rice makes good turkey stuffing, used half and half with ordinary long grain white rice.

Can you imagine something being salty, sweet, sour, and bitter at the same time? That is the best way to describe the sensation of chewing on specially preserved lemons, plums, lichees, and oranges. You may love them; you may feel like the top of your head is coming off. These dried fruits are Chinese-style munchies. A note: the red dates you see in every market, also called jujubes, are used only in cooking.

Red melon seeds, which are usually in the same section as the preserved fruits, are especially popular at New Year's (red is the color of happiness and prosperity), but they are available all the time. It's a real art getting the seed sideways between your teeth so that you can extract the meat.

There are dozens of varieties of tea. The Chinese call black tea "red" and *Pu-Erh* is one of the most popular. It has a musty flavor with lots of body. Luk-on is a soothing and delicate green tea that comes in little reusable baskets. If you are a big tea drinker, the flat plate-sized

63

CHINESE GROCERIES

Fish Balls Steam or stir-fry. Add a little water and some vegetables.

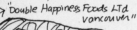

Fresh Noodles They are all available at the Double Happiness Factory. Many noodle houses sell fresh-made noodles also.

Bean Thread Noodles Soak before cooking or deep fry them as is.

Chinese Dried Mushrooms Soak again before cooking, and cut off the tough stems.

Peanuts Deep fry, and be careful not to burn them.

Preserved Vegetables This one is cured sui choy. Wash off the salt before using in a soup or for stir-frying.

packages of pressed black tea are the most economic buy.

For a different and special treat, why not try some of the canned fruits from the Orient? Chilled loquats, longans, or lichees make good snacks or desserts. The juice, served with ice, is a perfect summer drink.

And don't forget the candy. The White Rabbit brand from the People's Republic of China is by far the best seller and can be found everywhere. Chinese rice candies are chewy but not too sweet, and they are cheap. A huge box of Lucky Candy costs less than three dollars.

Most of the grocery stores also sell utensils and dishes in the back. If you are after everyday kitchenware, buy it here. The prices in the curio shops will be much higher. A small soup bowl might be seventy-five cents here, and a good-sized lidded rice bowl is usually under five dollars.

If you don't own a wok yet, make the investment. You can stir-fry, sauté, deep fry, steam, and simmer in this round-bottomed pot. Flat-bottomed woks are not recommended, as they need more oil, and the food burns easily because there is a larger area in direct contact with the burner. Don't buy fancy copper, brass, or stainless steel. A good heavy iron or carbon steel wok is best and costs less than fifteen dollars. Don't forget to pick up a curved spatula with your new wok, and one of the brass skimmers will be useful for removing pieces of food when you're deep frying.

The round bamboo baskets stack inside the wok for steaming foods. The latticework bottom lets the heat rise up three or four stories, if you are cooking several things, and a domed bamboo lid covers the top steamer. They come in various sizes and are priced from one to four dollars.

The clay pots bound with wire are used for stews and casserole-type dishes. The wire helps to distribute the heat evenly. The pots can be used on gas stoves or in the oven, but the heat from an electric element may be too direct and intense. The tall, thin clay pots with spouts on the side are used for making the sweet vinegar childbirth broth, and the lidded porcelain pots with the stubby handles on each side are for steaming herbal medicines.

In this section of the store you may also find incense, packages of colored paper, or what looks like play money. These are all religious items and are used as offerings to ancestors and various gods.

MORE GROCERIES

Shrimp Chips Pop the dried pastel chips into hot oil, and they puff up like magic.

(fried)

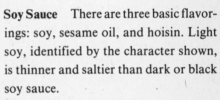

Soy Sauce There are three basic flavorings: soy, sesame oil, and hoisin. Light soy, identified by the character shown, is thinner and saltier than dark or black soy sauce.

Red Bean Paste Thick and sweet, this is the filling for many Chinese pastries.

Chinese Sausages Locally made, these have an international reputation and are often taken home by Hong Kong visitors as a souvenir.

Barbecued Meat, Fresh Poultry, and Live Fish

A Chinese butcher shop, like the **Dollar Market** (266 East Pender), tends to get crowded around 5:00 in the afternoon when there's no time to cook dinner. The answer is barbecued pork, chicken, or duck. No preparation is needed; just arrange it on a plate with a little rice and a stir-fried vegetable, and it's all done.

Cha siu (barbecued pork) is bought by the strip, by weight, or by the dollar. *Siu gap* and *siu gai* (barbecued duck and chicken) are bought by the half or the whole, and don't forget to take the sauce. The butcher will always cut the meat into bite-sized pieces. Try to eat the barbecued meat as soon as possible. If you have to keep it for a while before serving, refrigerate, then warm it in the oven or steam for a few minutes before serving.

You can also buy whole chickens stewed in soy sauce. The chicken wrapped in tissue paper has been baked Hakka-style in hot rock salt. The plain white steamed chickens complete with head and feet are often used for religious offerings. Fresh chicken is a specialty at **G. Mart Poultry Sales** (437 Gore).

You will also see row upon row of *lok chur* (Chinese sausages) hung in twos with red strings. These should be steamed first, or you can make a quick meal by cutting one or two into small pieces and stir-frying them with leftover rice.

The big *lop not* (flattened ducks) have been dried and will keep for ages. Cut off a small piece and place it on rice while it steams. The meat is rich and strong and makes a good meal on a cold winter night. Livers, tongues, lungs, and other organ meats are also available at these markets. Many Chinese have faith in sympathetic medicine; cow's stomach helps the digestion, brains make you smart, and chicken feet soothe aching arches.

Finally, if you want fresh beef, tell the butcher how you want to cook it. He will then select the right cut for stir-frying or soup-making. Chinatown meat is probably the freshest in town because butchers prefer to buy just what will be needed for the day.

Vancouver has lots of fish shops but nothing quite like the ones in Chinatown. At places like **Pender Seafoods** (284 East Pender) or **Hong Chong Fish** (209 East Pender) all the fish are sold whole, and you make your own selection after peering inside the gills with a long metal hook.

keefer Chinese Bakery, 217 keefer St.

THE BAKERY WINDOW

The window of the Keefer Bakery is one of the prettiest in Chinatown. The pastel colored cakes announce a wedding. When a girl gets engaged, her family distributes these to friends and relatives in the round lacquer boxes, which can be rented from the bakery.

Both shops also have live fish. The price is certainly higher, but freshness is guaranteed.

Bakery Row

For a long time, only a few varieties of buns, egg tarts, and ceremonial sweets were available in Chinatown. Don Lee opened the Hong Kong style **Keefer Street Bakery** (217 Keefer) in 1974. Within a few years **Loong Foong** (247 Keefer) and **Maxim's** (257 Keefer) had opened just up the street, and this former warehouse block is now Chinatown's bakery row.

Inside it's hard to distinguish one bakery from another, and the competition means that all three have to maintain high standards, so I divide my shopping between them.

You can start with the ubiquitous *cha siu bau* (barbecued pork buns) and then move on to the smaller buns and rolls filled with savory black bean, sweet red bean, or lotus paste. There are also pineapple buns, buns filled with butter and coconut cream, and buns filled with slices of ham and egg. There are coconut cupcakes, chewy sausage and peanut "cookies," and tiny sponge cakes shaped like miniature chef's hats.

The other side of the bakery looks like a French pastry shop. When China was opened to western trade after 1900, hotels sprang up to serve the foreign merchants. The kitchens were usually run by French chefs who brought their own style of baked goods. The Chinese modified the pastries, keeping the fancy decorations, but made them a little less sweet. The squares with jellolike tops are the Chinese version of trifle with sponge cake on the bottom, natural fruit filling in the middle, and a third layer of clear gelatin on top.

Wo Fat (30 East Hastings) doesn't look like a thriving bakery from the outside, but, for over sixty years, traditional Chinese cakes have been shipped all over Canada from this spot. Nobody seems to speak English here, but I have a friend who has been eating her way through the selection for years by just pointing. It's worth a visit.

Herbalists

Many visitors to Chinatown are puzzled by the herbal shops with their unusual window displays of dried seahorses or ground deer

Herbalist shop in Chinatown.

antlers. These are Chinese-style pharmacies, and there are half a dozen of them strung along Main and Pender Streets.

Traditional Chinese medicine is basically a balancing act between the forces of yin (cold) and yang (hot). The different parts of the body are in a yin and yang equilibrium. When the body is attacked by diseases (which are also identified as yin and yang), that balance is upset. The combination of roots, herbs, and animal parts prescribed by an herbalist will restore the patient to his natural yin and yang state.

The herbalist, who has the same relationship to the herbal doctor as a western pharmacist has to a medical doctor, stocks thousands of natural substances, including bear's stomach, snake skin, dried lizards, abalone shell, tree bark, and minerals. The herbalist grinds and combines these ingredients (usually according to a prescription) for poultices, ointment, or even pills, but most often, directions are given for boiling them up at home as teas or soups.

For common everyday ailments, the herbalist himself will often suggest a remedy. When I visisted Mr. Mak at **Dai Cheong** (254 East Pender), he suggested black bees preserved in salt for a sore throat. Many of these common remedies are available already prepared in bottles and boxes, and that's what you'll find on the shelves in the rest of the store.

Gift Shopping in Chinatown

People often forget Chinatown when they're looking for gifts. There is a lot of junk—endless mass-produced chains, tea sets, and paper lanterns. But with a little poking around in some of the smaller stores, you can find treasures that will have the most hardened cynic begging you to reveal your sources.

The **Chinese Cultural Centre** (50 East Pender) is a good place to start. For four dollars you can pick up a coloring book of folk dolls from China put together by a local couple, Alvin and Cecilia Chang. Nearby, the **Chinese Cultural Arts Centre** (20 East Pender) is actually a small gallery. The friendly owner will take time to explain that the stone rubbings are taken from ancestral tombs in China and suggest ways to mat his excellent selection of paper cuts.

Grand Jewellery (44 East Pender) has some unusual cloisonné pieces at good prices, and, for antiques, the **Great China Co.** (8 East

71

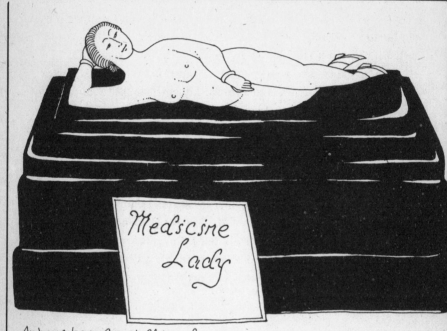

Antique box, Great China Co.

TRADITION IN MEDICINE

This ivory medicine lady was used by doctors in the old days. A Chinese woman was not expected to remove her clothing in the doctor's office. Instead, she would point to the medicine lady and indicate where her ailment was.

Pender) is your best bet. I have had mini tours from the young saleslady in this shop who will happily tell you the history of the ivory medicine lady or the old tea chest with the hidden drawers.

Across the street from the Cultural Centre, **Ming Wo's** at 23 East Pender now specializes in gourmet cookware and is known throughout the Lower Mainland by its shopping mall branches. Ming Wo's was originally a hardware store, and many of its most appealing items, like glassware and teapots, are from the restaurant supply line they have continued to carry.

China West (41 East Pender) is jammed floor to ceiling with an eclectic selection of clothes and trinkets. **Wah Yuen** (47 East Pender) is worth going into for the old mahogany and glass cases, which display china plates and hand-embroidered table linens. Two doors away, at 27 East Pender, **Chinese Linen and Silk** carries silks by the yard in colors and patterns that can't be found elsewhere in Vancouver.

At **Universal Art** (49 East Pender) you will find an unusual selection of paintings, ceramics, and old books. The best bargains are the miniature colored woodcuts, over one hundred years old, and priced under ten dollars. The owner, Lloyd Yee, is an artist himself and sells his own original brush paintings in the store.

I always go into **Gim Lee Yuen** (75 East Pender) because it smells so good. It's probably rose incense, which costs twenty-five cents a packet. Check the old display case in the center of the shop for special bargains. On one visit I saw a blue and white dinner set for twelve priced just over four hundred dollars.

Like many of the old stores on this block **Transnation Emporium** (89 East Pender) has a little herbalist shop at the back. Transnation is the place for dishes and tea sets. Those baskets lined with cotton insulation and fitted with a pot and several cups are actually a thermos system to keep your tea hot all day.

Oriental Importers (149 East Pender) has the feeling of an old dry goods store. Look around for good prices on silk blouses and women's and children's oriental pajamas. On my last visit, a dramatic hand-embroidered silk empress coat was very reasonably priced at just over one hundred dollars.

Perlin Music (107 East Pender) is one of the newest stores in Chinatown and carries a full range of beautiful though expensive handmade traditional Chinese musical instruments.

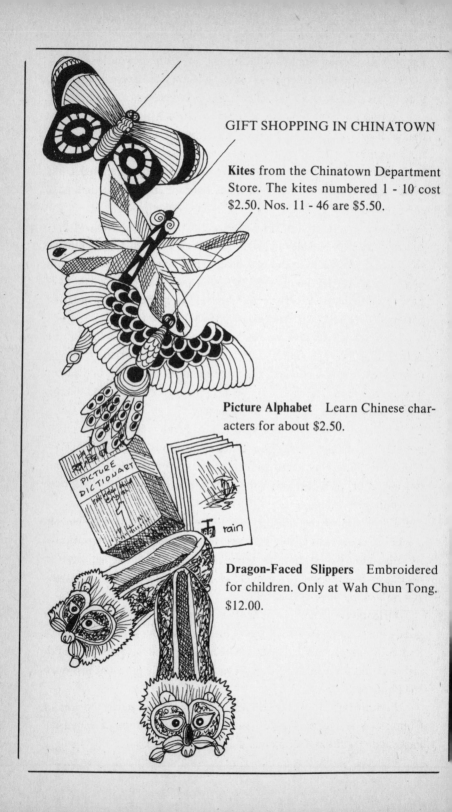

GIFT SHOPPING IN CHINATOWN

Kites from the Chinatown Department Store. The kites numbered 1 - 10 cost $2.50. Nos. 11 - 46 are $5.50.

Picture Alphabet   Learn Chinese characters for about $2.50.

Dragon-Faced Slippers   Embroidered for children. Only at Wah Chun Tong. $12.00.

If you're looking for toys or inexpensive party favors, Chinatown is the right place. The **Temple Shoppe, Wun San,** the **Chinatown Department Store, Gemway Arts and Crafts, Onward Trading,** and **N&S Trading Company** are clustered together in the middle of the one hundred block like a group of gold mines. Big wooden swords cost less than two dollars, and a game of Chinese checkers is only a few pennies more. The Temple Shoppe is the only place I've seen Chinese multicolored "thinking caps," and kids will love the tiny wooden tea sets at Wun San. Both items are under five dollars.

For someone with an offbeat sense of humor, the bamboo ear picks and plastic tongue scratchers at Onward Trading are fun. The tiny models of Chinese opera masks cost less than five dollars and are quite beautiful. Don't forget to go upstairs at the Chinatown Department Store for a look at the elaborate, gold-embroidered, tapestrylike center-pieces. They can be easily framed, and prices run from five to fifty dollars.

At the northwest corner of Pender and Main, **Chung Kiu** is probably the fanciest gift shop in Chinatown, with a wide selection of ceramics, enamelled jewelry, and elegant silk *cheong sam* dresses with mandarin collars.

Across Main, **Wah Chung Tong Enterprises** (207 East Pender) has items you won't find anywhere else in Chinatown. The large selection of ritual goods includes complete sets of paper clothing, small shrines, and incense burners. Wah Chung also carries dark, unglazed *I shing* pottery and is the only place I have found the traditional clay charcoal stoves used in China. They're perfect for outdoor barbecuing.

There are two or three jewelry stores as you go south along Main Street, and they are all filled with gold. You'll look in vain for price tags in places like **Wah Kiu Jewellers** (504 Main) because precious metal is sold by the daily market value. If you want Chinese jade, look for the lighter translucent shades of green. The dark green opaque jade is probably from British Columbia.

In **Van China Trade Centre** at the corner of Main and Keefer most of the inventory comes from the People's Republic of China, and here is where you will find the best selection of Chinese cosmetics, Pearl Dental

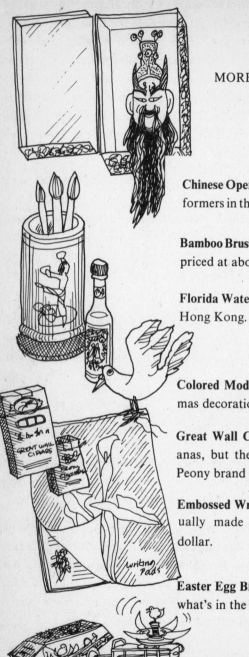

Chinese Opera Mask   Painted-face performers in the opera use these as models.

Bamboo Brush Holder   You'll find these priced at about $2.50.

Florida Water   Girl Brand comes from Hong Kong. Under a dollar.

Colored Model Birds   Use for Christmas decorations or present wrapping.

Great Wall Cigars   They're not Havanas, but they're worth a try. Or try Peony brand cigarettes.

Embossed Writing Pads   These are usually made of rice paper. Under a dollar.

Easter Egg Bird   Push the rod and see what's in the egg. Kids love it.

Cream, Butterfly Shaving Cream, and fifty-cent eyebrow/eyeliner pencils that last forever.

Music, Art, and Movies

The Chinese Cultural Centre has a mandate to involve the whole community in traditional arts and crafts. Non-Chinese are welcome to enrol in Cantonese and Mandarin language classes and courses in Chinese brush painting. *T'ai chi* classes are also available. A photographic history of the local Chinese community is on permanent display upstairs at the Cultural Centre, and the gallery next door has rotating exhibitions that often feature local Chinese-Canadian artists. The ladies group at the Centre offers tours of Chinatown. These can be arranged for in advance.

The Cultural Centre sponsors Chinese cultural events like the Shanghai Ballet, the Chinese Circus, and the Peking Opera. Often the opera gets assistance from local musicians who play traditional instruments. You can make arrangements to sit in on the rehearsals of the Chinese Instrumental Music Group, which practices every Sunday afternoon at the Cultural Centre.

The Strathcona Community Centre in the heart of the residential area at 601 Keefer has a full martial arts program. And it's well worth putting your little girl's name on the waiting list for Mimi Lee's Saturday classes in traditional Chinese folk dances. The Community Centre publishes a quarterly brochure with information about upcoming events. Telephone: 254-9496.

There are three Chinese movie theaters downtown, the **Golden Harvest** at 319 Main, and the **Shaw** and the **Sun Sing,** both on East Hastings (254 and 150). Hong Kong is one of the world's major movie capitals, and enough films are produced every year to keep all the theaters well supplied with new bills every couple of weeks. Many are subtitled in English, but you should call first. The flicks are usually light or comic romances like "Chasing Girls," or bad-guy pictures like "Legal Illegals," with lots of Kung Fu action.

Festivals and Holidays

The Canadian government has been talking for years about a midwinter holiday for the country. Why not adopt the ready-made Chinese New Year celebrations?

SIU MAI

(Steamed shrimp and pork pastries)

Sui mai is a basic dim sum dish. It is very easy and makes a good appetizer of lunch dish.

You will need: 1 pkg won ton skins

½ kg (1 lb.) of fresh shrimp, cleaned, deveined, and chopped coarsely

½ kg (1 lb.) of ground pork

Mix all ingredients (except won ton skins) well. Refrigerate if you are not going to use immediately.

Trim won ton skins into a circle. Put a tablespoon of filling on each round. Fold skin around filling, then squeeze the middle around the waistline. Pack filling and flatten bottom. Grease steamer; arrange the siu mai and steam over boiling water for about twelve minutes.

Serve with a soy oil dip of four parts dark soy sauce to one part sesame oil.

The Chinese have a lunar calendar, and the new year comes on the second new moon after the winter solstice, usually in late January. Also called the Spring Festival, this is a family celebration that marks a time of renewal. All debts are settled before the first day of the new year, the herbalists close their doors because it is bad luck to start the year with sickness, and some of the old people still put their brooms away and let their hair get dirty in the first few days of the new year, so that good luck won't be swept or washed away. These are the best days of the year for children, who receive red packages filled with *lishee* (lucky money) from married people.

During the New Year's activities, the Chinese Cultural Centre sponsors a flower market and a lantern workshop for kids, and on the weekend of the parade there are many displays and demonstrations.

Most of Chinatown is cordoned off for the lion dance, which is usually planned for the first weekend after New Year's Day. Dozens of family associations and athletic groups participate, each with their own papier maché lion, which kung fu dancers hoist on their shoulders and carry through the streets.

Shop owners attract the lion to their door with offerings of lishee and lettuce, a lucky vegetable. The higher the lion has to reach for the offerings, the more luck and prosperity the business will have. Drummers accompany the lion to encourage him in his feats, and everybody throws firecrackers to ward off evil spirits. The dragon, nearly a hundred feet long and the symbol of goodness and strength, may or may not make an appearance, depending on his mood. You'll just have to go and find out.

Every family has a special dinner at home on New Year's Eve, and most have one more banquet at a restaurant during the following week. The special New Year's dishes like *Faat Choy Ho Zee* (oysters with rock hair) will not be on the menu, but the kitchen will be happy to serve them if you ask. Each of these dishes represent a wish for prosperity in the new year; for example, the character for *faat choy* means "an increase in wealth." The traiditional toast at New Year's is *gung hei faat choy*.

Although moon cakes are now sold year-round, they are mainly associated with the midautumn festival held on the fifteenth day of the eighth lunar month. Traditionally this celebration marked the harvest and honored the moon goddess, who was at her fullest this time of year.

During the Yuan dynasty, when the Mongol rulers were particularly oppressive to the Han Chinese, the moon cakes took on new significance. Messages were concealed in the circular cakes, advising the people that the time for rebellion had come, and the secret signal was the lighting of the lanterns during the harvest festival. On August 15, A.D. 1366, the Chinese people rose up and broke the rule of the invaders, and the period of the Ming dynasty began.

The golden moon cakes, stamped with an intricate design, are too difficult to make at home, so local bakeries are crowded. The cakes have a filling of sweet lotus seed or bean paste and sometimes the yolk of a salted egg. The lions also come out for the Moon Festival, and there is usually a good-sized parade down Pender Street.

There are a couple of stories of the origin of the Dragon Boat Festival, which comes in late spring, but both involve a brave man who drowned himself in the river. In one story, he is protesting corruption; in the other story, he commits suicide when falsely accused of treason by the emperor's son. Dragon boats race to a designated spot in a river with specially wrapped rice dumplings, which, according to tradition, either scare the sharks away from the drowned body or, in the second version, on the order of the repentant emperor, feed the drowned man's spirit.

In Vancouver, the occasion is marked by a traditional sweet. The *jung* are easily recognized by their dried bamboo leaf wrapper. The rice filling can be savory or sweet. The sweet ones are made by soaking the rice in lye water. Like moon cakes, jung are now sold year-round and there is always a display in the window of Yip Hong Yuen. Don't forget that the leaf is just a container and is not to be eaten.

The Ching Ming Festival, in the third lunar month, is not celebrated as extensively as it used to be, but many older Chinese take this opportunity to visit the graves of ancestors and make special offerings. Paper representations of clothing and money are burned on the altar, along with small offerings of food. There's a special Chinese shrine used for Ching Ming in the Fraserview Cemetary just north of 33rd and Fraser.

Around Town

It is so difficult to get a parking spot in Chinatown, especially on the weekends, that many Chinese-Canadians give up and patronize the many excellent Chinese restaurants around town, especially for regional styles of cooking.

The *New York Times* has recommended **Yang's** at 25th and Main. On Saturday mornings the chef makes his own noodles right in the middle of the restaurant. For dessert, at this northern restaurant, try the carmellized banana and apple slices. They're deep fried first and then dunked in cold water at your table.

For spicy Szechuan food, try either of the two **Snow Garden** restaurants at 50th and Main (in the heart of Little India) or at 513 West Pender. The **Shanghai Paramount** (2550 Kingsway) gets raves for its eastern food, and so does **Vong's Kitchen,** a little hole-in-the-wall at 5989 Fraser Street always packed with faithful customers.

The **Kingsland** is the most popular banquet hall outside Chinatown. The location on Granville Mall is convenient, and the decor is rich with reds, greens, and golds. The **Miramar** (2046 West 41st) has a good dim sum reputation, and for an authentic New Year's feast, try the **Flamingo** (7510 Cambie).

The **Asian Centre** at UBC has regular lunchtime programs of films and lectures, many of them on Chinese themes. And they have regular conversation classes for those who wish to keep practicing their Cantonese or Mandarin.

The Museum of Anthropology, in conjunction with the Department of Continuing Education, has many Chinese artifacts and regularly offers Exploring Chinatown courses with curator Betsy Johnson, who speaks Cantonese and is an excellent guide to the ins and outs of the Chinese food stores and restaurants.

If You Want to Know More

The community now supports three daily Chinese language newspapers, but only the biweekly *Chinatown News* is published in English. It is a good source of information about what's happening in the community and carries articles on local politics, festivals, and cultural events. A subscription costs ten dollars per year and can be ordered from the Chinatown News at 459 East Hastings Street.

Another effective way to keep in touch with what's going on is through the *Mainstreet Magazine*, published quarterly by the Chinese Cultural Center. The address is 50 East Pender Street (687-0729).

Also at the Cultural Centre you can find a set of pamphlets called China in Chinatown put together by a group of local young Chinese Canadians. A set of four costs three dollars and covers subjects like traditional Chinese music or local Chinatown history.

West Coast Chinese Boy by Sing Lim published by Tundra books in 1975 is a perfect introduction for children (and adults) to the early days of the Chinese community remembered by an artist who grew up in Canton Alley in the 'teens and 'twenties of this century. The beautiful glass plate prints are by the author. *Opening Doors, Vancouver's East End,* edited by Daphne Marlatt and Carole Itter, Sound Heritage Series, published by the Provincial Archives of B.C., Volume VIII, nos. 1 and 2, is another treasure book filled with personal interviews with many of the old timers who have seen Chinatown grow from a few shacks on False Creek to a city within the city.

Vancouver has the second largest Chinatown in North America, and new shops and restaurants are opening every month. It takes far more than one afternoon to explore it all, so you have plenty of adventures awaiting you. Have fun.

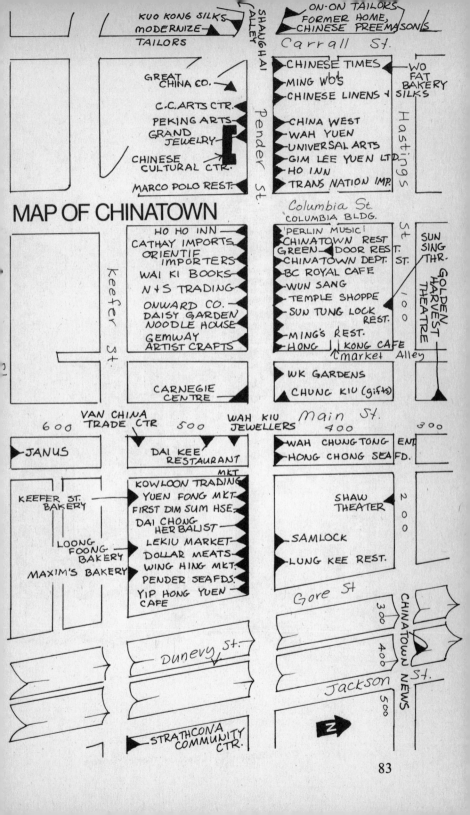

MAP OF CHINATOWN

KUO KONG SILKS
MODERNIZE
TAILORS

SHANGHAI ALLEY

ON-ON TAILORS
FORMER HOME,
CHINESE PREEMASONS

Carrall St.

GREAT CHINA CO.

C.C. ARTS CTR.
PEKING ARTS
GRAND JEWELRY

CHINESE CULTURAL CTR.

MARCO POLO REST.

Pender St.

CHINESE TIMES
MING WO'S
CHINESE LINENS

CHINA WEST
WAH YUEN
UNIVERSAL ARTS
GIM LEE YUEN LTD.
HO INN
TRANS NATION IMP.

WO FAT BAKERY
SILKS

Hastings

Columbia St.
COLUMBIA BLDG.

HO HO INN
CATHAY IMPORTS
ORIENTIF IMPORTERS
WAI KI BOOKS
N+S TRADING
ONWARD CO.
DAISY GARDEN
NOODLE HOUSE
GEMWAY
ARTIST CRAFTS

Keefer St.

PERLIN MUSIC
CHINATOWN REST
GREEN DOOR REST.
CHINATOWN DEPT. ST.
BC ROYAL CAFE
WUN SANG
TEMPLE SHOPPE
SUN TUNG LOCK REST.
MING'S REST.
HONG KONG CAFE

market Alley

St. 100

SUN SING THR.

GOLDEN HARVEST THEATRE

CARNEGIE CENTRE

WK GARDENS
CHUNG KIU (gifts)

VAN CHINA
TRADE CTR

600   500

WAH KIU
JEWELLERS

Main St.
400   300

JANUS

DAI KEE RESTAURANT
MKT

KOWLOON TRADING
YUEN FONG MKT.
FIRST DIM SUM HSE.
DAI CHONG HERBALIST
LEKIU MARKET
DOLLAR MEATS
WING HING MKT.
PENDER SEAFDS.
YIP HONG YUEN CAFE

WAH CHUNG TONG   ENT
HONG CHONG SEA   FD.

KEEFER ST. BAKERY

LOONG FOONG BAKERY

MAXIM'S BAKERY

SHAW THEATER

SAMLOCK

LUNG KEE REST.

200

Gore St.

CHINATOWN NEWS St.

300

400

Dunevy St.

Jackson

500

STRATHCONA COMMUNITY CTR.

E

83

The Sikh Temple, 8000 Ross St. (Ross at Marine Drive)

LITTLE INDIA

Most people know where Chinatown is and that Powell Street is the center of Japanese shopping. Commercial Drive is Italian, and West Broadway is the place for Greek stores and restaurants. But Little India? Most Vancouverites draw a blank, although the sixty thousand Indo-Canadians in the city form one of our largest ethnic groups.

Head up Main Street to where it intersects with 49th Avenue, and you'll find yourself on the high street of a typical Punjabi town. The Indian community has historically centered itself in South Vancouver close to the lumber mills of the Fraser River, and this part of Main Street is the core shopping area; in fact, local merchants recently dubbed it the Punjabi Market in 1982.

The shop hours are flexible here; many stay open well after 6:00 p.m. on weekdays. On weekends the market starts bustling early in the morning. The men gather to talk on the street corners, and the women crowd into the saree stores or tempt themselves with the 22-carat gold ornaments at the jewelry shops. The sweet shops have take-out snacks and desserts, and in the groceries you can find everything from saffron to the latest movie magazines from India.

Sikhs, Hindus, and Muslims

The largest number of Indians in Vancouver come from the northwest section of the Punjab province on the boundary with Pakistan. The Punjab is the home of Sikhism, a relatively new religion that had its beginnings in the late fifteenth century, initially as a response to the caste oppression of Hinduism and later as a result of the economic and political repression of the Mongol (Muslim) invaders from Persia.

Punjabi and Sikh are, however, not interchangeable terms. Many Muslims remained in the Punjab, although Indian Independence had created a separate Muslim state in Pakistan. Thus, an immigrant from the Punjab could well be Muslim (or, for that matter, Hindu or

85

Christian). Muslims—about three thousand in Vancouver—are followers of Islam, a monotheistic religion much like Judaism or Christianity. Mohammed is held to be the last in a line of prophets that includes both Moses and Jesus. Many of the Indian familes who emigrated to Africa belong to the Ismaili sect of the Muslim religion, led by the international philanthropist, the Aga Khan. Several thousand Asian Africans settled in Vancouver after Idi Amin's expulsion order of 1972.

Although seventy percent of the Indians living in Vancouver are Sikh, Hinduism is the oldest and strongest religion in India. For Hindus there is one all-encompassing divine spirit who appears in various incarnations representing aspects of his personality. Vishnu, the preserver of good, and Shiva, the destroyer of evil, are the two principal deities. Vishnu's wife, Lakshmi, the goddess of prosperity, and Shiva's elephant-headed son Ganesh, who exemplifies prudence, are two of many others. Many immigrants from the south of India are Hindus.

The local community also includes Parsees, followers of the Zoroastrian religion whose ancestors were exiled from Persia and settled in Bombay. Finally, Christianity had a fair rate of success in India, and about twelve million are believers in the teachings of the New Testament.

A Walking Tour of Little India

You can start your walking tour of Little India at 48th Avenue and Main, although this block is just beginning to develop an Indian character. South of 49th is where the market really begins. It's just two short blocks, but they are jammed on both sides with food stores, saree shops, and restaurants.

Unless you're feeling very energetic, it's probably best to drive to the Ross Street Temple. There are thirteen Sikh temples in Vancouver, but this one, at the corner of Marine Drive and Ross Street, is the biggest and most outstanding. The award-winning design by Arthur Erickson includes a main hall that can accommodate two thousand with a gallery for three hundred more. Skylights in the stepped ceiling give the hall a natural glow that is made even richer by thick red carpets and the bright red colors of the women's clothes. The exterior of the building is angular, made of white stone, and crowned with an open ribbed golden dome.

The best time to visit the temple is in the early evening, particularly on a Friday, between 6:30 and 8:00 p.m. Services consist of spoken passages from the beautiful Sikh holy book, the *Guru Granth*. Every weekend it is read aloud from beginning to end by members of the temple. You can go in anytime and stay as long as you wish, but you must remove your shoes at the entrance, and both men and women must cover their heads.

Downstairs there is a huge dining room, which can feed four hundred in one sitting. Vegetarian meals are prepared throughout the weekend, and visitors are always graciously welcomed.

Indian Food

There are many different styles of Indian cooking, largely determined by geography and religion. For example, Indian food is not always hot. The original function of spices was to preserve foods. In the north, where the temperatures can be very cold, the food is mildly spiced. It's farther south toward Madras, where freshly killed meat can putrefy in a couple of hours, that the art of combining strong spices has been perfected.

Nor is Indian food exclusively vegetarian. True, it is against the Hindu religion to slaughter cows (Lord Krishna, another incarnation of Vishnu, spent his boyhood as a cowherd and saw the whole cosmos reflected in the body of a cow), and upper-caste Hindus have evolved a very sophisticated diet that excludes all meat, fish, poultry, eggs, and shellfish. But the other twenty percent of the population (about seventy million) have no religious rules against the consumption of beef. Muslims do not eat pork, but their reputation for cooking lamb and goat (usually called mutton) is unequaled. And in the Punjab, among Sikhs, red meat and chicken are an important part of the northern diet.

Northern-style cooking predominates in most Indian restaurants and homes in North America. This is the most celebrated of Indian regional styles, much of it influenced by the Mogul kings (you'll see that name *Mogul* again and again on Indian menus). Originally Mongol-Turks, they first came through Persia in the twelfth century, establishing a Muslim kingdom on the northern plains near Delhi. With them the Moguls brought a sensuousness and a love of splendor that is reflected in their silky yogurt sauces, rich meat preparations, and elaborately layered rice dishes. The Mogul spices are fragrant, with lots of

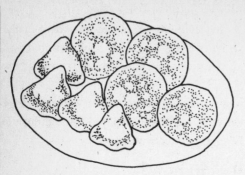

Samosas and matthi

INDIAN SNACKS AND DESSERTS

Samosas These are triangular-shaped pastries stuffed with meat or vegetables.

Matthi This popular snack food is usually served before dinner with drinks.

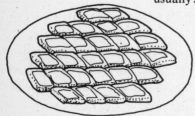

burfee

Burfees They're made from milk that has been reduced over low heat. The best burfees are soft and not too sweet.

Jalebis Made from all purpose flour, butter, and sugar, these are the most popular Indian sweet.

jalebis

cinnamon, cardamom, nutmeg, and cloves.

The word "curry," by the way, is not in the Indian vocabulary. It is a British pronunciation of *kari*, a green aromatic plant whose leaves were used in flavoring southern dishes. But the British adopted the term to describe any dish cooked in a spicy sauce. The important word to know as far as spicing goes is *masala*. Masalas are the mixtures of spices that form the basis of the flavoring for particular dishes.

Pakoras to Paans: A Guide to a Typical Indian Menu

Of all the ethnic food described in this book, Indian meals are probably the most unfamiliar. So here's a simple guide from appetizer to dessert for the next time you're eating out at an Indian restaurant. (Most of these dishes are northern, although there are occasional regional specialties.)

Let's start with appetizers. *Samosas* (one of the few foods eaten all over India) are deep-fried turnovers filled with spiced ground meat or served vegetarian-style with potatoes and peas. *Pakoras* are spicy vegetable fritters a little like Japanese tempura. Paper thin *pappadums* are plate-sized wafers that come spiced or plain. Soup was not a traditional part of an Indian meal until the British came along and helped invent spicy *mulligawtawny*, now a featured item on most menus.

Meat dishes may include lamb, beef, or goat, if it is available. *Kheemas* are made from ground meat and are like a chili dish without the beans. *Koftas* are meatballs. Small chunks of braised meat are cooked with thick yogurt sauces to make rich *kormas*. *Biryani* dishes combine chicken, beef, lamb, or vegetables with fragrant, long-grain *basmati rice*. They are often flavored with saffron and decorated with nuts and fruits. These dishes are completely different from the everyday *pullau*, which is basically plain rice with the meat or vegetable additions taking second place.

The most popular poultry delight is *tandoori* chicken. A whole bird is marinated in yogurt and spices and then cooked in an outdoor clay oven where the juices are sealed in a crispy exterior, which is colored deep orange from a liberal lacing of tumeric.

Since the Punjab is landlocked, fish dishes are rare. Although India does have thousands of miles of coastland, popular fish like *vekti* or

THE THALI DINNER

Traditional *thali* dinners are served in several local restaurants. On the stainless steel thali tray or plate, several matching *katori* bowls are filled with individual portions of meat, vegetables, and dahls. The roti can be your utensils. Daubs of chutney or pickles are always placed in the center of the thali.

eleesh aren't usually available in this part of the world. But the *pomfret* is similar enough to sole, and our large prawns are much like Indian *choto gheenjari*. In local restaurants, they are often prepared in pungent west coast Goanese style.

Aside from meatless koftas or biryanis, vegetarian dishes will include *dahls*—any of a dozen varieties of dried beans or peas steamed or pureed and delicately flavored—and *panir*, the only Indian cheese. Made from cow or buffalo milk, panir is drier than Italian ricotta and is especially popular in the north, cooked with greens.

There are all kinds of regional rules about whether *roti* (bread) and rice can be eaten together, but in North American homes and restaurants both are usually on the table. The different kinds of roti can be confusing at first. The round, flat, unleavened *chapati* is the most common. Deep-fried *puris*, which puff up like shower caps, are smaller and lighter. *Parathas* are often square or rectangular in shape, a little crispy, and slightly flaky. They are cooked on a griddle something like a pancake. The teardrop-shaped *naan* or rounded *kulcha* is cooked on the inside wall of a tandoori oven and rises about three centimeters; they are the only leavened Indian breads. All of these breads have a double function as utensils to scoop up food. You don't need knives and forks when you have roti—just tear off small pieces and wrap them around rice or meat. You can mix your rice and dahl together with the tips of your fingers, but to be authentic, go no farther than the second knuckle and use only your right hand.

Most restaurant desserts don't go much farther than spongy *gulab jamans* (a lot like rum babas). The real delights are found in the local sweet shops.

If you want something to drink with your Indian meal, iced fruit drinks or *sharbats* are traditional. The strong flavors of most Indian foods will drown out delicate wines, so fairly hearty reds are your best bet. My perference is beer, which has just the right edge for spicy food. If you don't want alcohol, *llassi*, a rose-flavored yogurt drink, is delicious. *Kachi llassi* is a bit thinner, made from water and a little fresh milk, usually flavored with *kawra,* which tastes like sage. *Cha* (Indian tea) is spiced with cinnamon and nutmeg and comes with lots of milk. Coffee is also a popular drink in India.

Finally, to refresh your mouth and aid digestion, try a *paan*. The equivalent of an after-dinner mint, the fancy ones have nippy seeds and

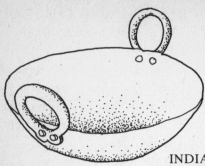

INDIAN COOKWARE

Karhai or Kadai For deep frying. Shaped like a Chinese wok, it can be made of cast iron, aluminum, stainless steel, or brass.

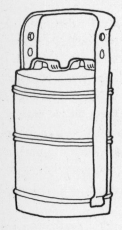

Tiftin Carrier This is the convenient Indian lunchbox with two completely separate compartments.

Tokara Stacked aluminum trays for steaming several different dishes at once.

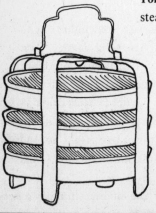

nuts mixed with a lime paste and are wrapped in a fresh betel leaf. Just let it sit in your mouth while the flavors slowly develop. If the rolled paan isn't available, every restaurant will have a paan box or dish with a loose assortment of sugar-coated or plain fennel seeds, whole carda-moms, or sweet or plain betel nuts.

A Restaurant Guide to the Punjabi Market

If you ask an Indian to suggest a good restaurant, he will probably shake his head. It is not that he's keeping a secret; the general opinion seems to be that nothing beats home cooking. That may well be true, but there are some good Indian restaurants in Vancouver, and they're getting better all the time. In the past year some really impressive new places have opened, and two of them are in the Punjabi Market.

The **India Palace** (6633 Main) has lots of atmosphere, with red carpets, chandeliers, and big fan-shaped rattan chairs. Chef Gurupal Singh is proud of his southern-style dishes, particularly the *Masala Dosa*, a pastry covered casserole stuffed with potatoes, meat, and hot peppers. And do try their hand-rolled paans. There's also dancing on weekend evenings.

The **Moti Mahal** is expensive, but, for a special night out, it's worth it. There are some really unusual dishes here, like parathas stuffed with meat or chicken. Owner Blawant Kainth and his wife have a long history in the restaurant business, both in the Punjab and now in Canada. The Moti Mahal is their second restaurant in the Main street area. They are also the proprietors of **Raja's Tandoori Hut** farther south at 7271 Main. The tandoori chicken in this little place is excellent, the prices are very low, and the service is always friendly.

If you prefer to stay at home, the Tandoori Hut will also deliver for a minimum order of thirty dollars. The Kainths also run Modern Party Rentals and Catering Services up the street at 7209 Main and will do it all for you, from renting the chairs to supplying tandoori chicken for five hundred.

The **Himalaya** (6595 Main) is never going to win any awards for fine dining, but I like eating here because it's right in the middle of the Market and has the best view of the street. This is definitely where the locals eat, especially the young single men. The food is basic, inexpensive, and filling.

93

6681 Main Street

THE MARKET PLACE

The Main Food Centre is one of several groceries in the Punjabi Market. As well as Indian specialties, these stores are good places to buy staples such as flour, sugar, and oil. Fierce price cutting among all the stores means low prices for shoppers.

A Shopping Tour of the Punjabi Market

Until quite recently, many of the Indian shops were scattered along Fraser Street. But higher rents and a determination by local business-men to build a strong commercial core for the community resulted in the unified Punjabi Market Association and a shopping area that can now truly be described as a little bit of India. New shops are opening every month, and it's always a colorful place to visit.

There are a number of unusual features to this market area. The first you'll probably notice is the large number of saree shops—twelve in two blocks at last count. Surprisingly, most sarees are not bought for wear in Vancouver. Three-quarters of the sarees and fabric lengths for Punjabi-style ladies' trouser suits are bought as gifts for friends and relatives back home. Even though most of the material is imported from Asia or the Orient, it is still high status in India to receive such a gift from North America.

Even in this very small area many of the stores have branches. There are two Guru Bazaars, for example, and the Japan Saree House is a subsidiary of the Frontier Cloth House. So if a salesperson suggests you try the store across the street, she may not be sending you to the competition at all. Price cutting among all the stores is also fierce, and for consumers it means lots of bargains (the mark-up of fabrics is sometimes as low as twenty-five per cent.

The Food Stores

At the Punjabi Market you can divide up your shopping list and try out most of the stores. The **Main Food Store** at 6681 Main has an excellent selection of fresh vegetables and the widest assortment of cooking utensils. Owner Chris Duggal, who also owns the India Palace restaurant, is always helpful. The big portraits all around the store are of the ten Sikh gurus. In a Hindi-owned store you'll usually find a brightly-colored relief wall plaque of one of the gods or goddesses.

The **Chauhan Grocery** just across the street (6684 Main) was one of the first food stores in the area. **J&B Foods** at 6607 Main stocks as many Canadian goods as well as Indian imports but does have excellent prices. The **India Supermarket** (6438 Main) is the newest grocery in the area. It still has a warehouse feel to it, and you can scoop spices straight out of the big cardboard shipping barrels.

Comparison shopping is well worth the time it takes. Each

eggplant
bangan

okra

bora
beans

Kari
leaves

Patels
Curry Leaves

chilis

GROCERIES

Bangan (eggplant) It can be roasted, fried, and stuffed. The Indian eggplant is less bitter and doesn't need peeling.

Okra Snap the pods to make sure they are young and crisp.

Bora Beans From Fiji.

Kari Leaves Used especially to make hot west coast Goanese masalas.

Chilis To remove the seed from red and green chilis, break the pod in half and brush out the seeds with your fingers.

merchant will claim his are the lowest prices, but I like **Globe Spices** (6596 Main) and found the vehement claims of Mrs. Swali hard to resist. The Punjabi Market is, by the way, the best place to stock up on staples like flour, sugar, and oil, as prices are often thirty to forty percent cheaper than those of regular supermarkets.

From Ghee to Jackfruit: Shopping at an Indian Food Store

The air is full of the aroma of dozens of spices, and your nose is the first thing that starts working when you step inside the door of an Indian food store. You will probably recognize *dalchini* (cinnamon), *tej patta* (bay leaves), *mirch* (chili powder), and *laung* (whole cloves). You will also find *dhaniya* (brown coriander seeds), and *zeera* (cumin), both of which are used in practically every Indian dish. Vegetarian dishes always need *methi* (fenugreek), and, if you're looking for *emli* (tamarind), it often comes in a pressed bar that has to be soaked first to release the juicy pulp. *Heeng* is a gummy resin that adds an oniony flavor, and green and white *ilaighi* (cardamoms) are not just for cooking. The greens ones are especially good sucked whole as a breath freshener.

You can buy many ready-made masalas for meat and fish, but, for the traditional hot garam masala, it's best to grind your own. You can experiment later with proportions, but try starting with 100 grams (four ounces) of coriander seeds; 50 grams (two ounces) each of cumin, peppercorns, and large cardamoms, plus 25 grams (one ounce) of cinnamon and 25 grams (1 ounce) of cloves.

Among the oils you'll find, *ghee* (clarified butter) is the main cooking medium, and the yellow bottles are easy to identify. Palm oil is used in East African cooking, and, for making pickles, mustard oil is what you want. Castor oil is used for hair tonic, and many westerners use coconut oil for suntanning.

Try a package of *pappadums*. They puff up in seconds on a hot grill, or they can be quickly deep fried. Those little pastel-colored dried chips flavored with cumin can also be deep-fried for another treat. You need just a little hot oil for cooking up rice flakes. Add some peanuts, cashews, a little salt, chili powder, and a bit of tumeric, and you've got a fast and favorite Indian breakfast.

Some of the stores carry dried strips of Bombay duck, which is not

MORE GROCERIES

Tamarind   The edible pulp of the tamarind seed pod is used in Indian cooking for its special acid sweet taste. Dried tamarind has to be soaked to separate out the pulp. The instant powdered variety is less authentic but saves time.

Masalas   There are many ready-made masalas for certain types of dishes, like layered rice and meat biryanis.

Pappadums   These come in several sizes and different flavors, from plain to hot and spicy with garlic and red and green chilis. Deep fry them in oil or toast on a grill. Try them with a little mango chutney or mango pickles.

Dried Panir   Soak this Indian "cheese" in milk and sautée lightly.

Dried Burriyan   An instant "curry" dish. Add a little water and fry.

duck at all but a flat fish found off the west coast of India. It must be soaked overnight first and, until it's cooked, has quite an unpleasant odor. But the finished dish is one of the great Indian delicacies.

The variety of dahls is overwhelming. *Chana dahl* (hulled and split gram beans), and *masoor dahl* (tiny salmon-colored beans that turn yellow when they're cooked) are two of the more common ones. Of course each has its own flavor and cooking style, and dahls are not interchangeable in recipes. Dahls are also ground into flours.

More decisions must be made when you come to the *chutneys* and pickles. Both are condiments, the chutneys usually thicker and sweeter than the pickles. The only rule is contrast. If your main dishes are mild, go for a hot pickle. Cool chutneys can counterbalance something very spicy.

Most of the canned foods are imported and are fairly expensive, but you might give *patra* a try. This cabbage-type roll comes spiced and ready to eat. Corned mutton from Australia is another Indian favorite. It can be warmed up and eaten as is, or fried with chopped onions and fresh green chili peppers.

Nearby the bottles of sliced ripe mangoes or passion fruit are a treat on ice cream, or add a little sugar and water, get out the blender, and make a drink. The cans of tropical fruit juices like lichee or guava are sweet, but chilled they are very refreshing.

In the vegetable section you'll find *hari dhania* (leafy green coriander) and *dollo* (taro root). The huge black *nigos* (yams) are used for potato and curry dishes. Lo-bok (called daikon in Japan) is *mooli* in India. This root vegetable will grow anywhere, and Punjabi farmers often use it to fill in the corners of their fields. Bright green *bhindi* (okra), shaped like a tiny ribbed banana, is probably the most popular Indian vegetable. Sliced into rounds, bhindi can be steamed, lightly sautéed, or even deep fried. *Bangan* (Indian eggplants) are long, thin, and bright purple, not at all like the pear-shaped European variety, and the taste is different enough to make them worth trying.

Beware of green chilis. The smaller they are, the hotter they get. It is the seeds that really burn, so if you want to be safe, remove them and just use the pod for flavoring.

A slice of fresh green mango makes an instant condiment that adds tartness to your meal. And if you want to drink the milk of a coconut,

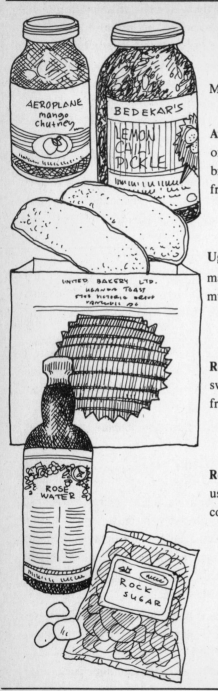

MORE GROCERIES

Aeroplane and Bedekar's   These are two of the most popular chutney and pickle brands. There are dozens more to choose from.

Uganda Toast   Dry and rusk-like, it's made locally for the East African community.

Rose Water   Used for flavoring many sweets. (Western women use it as a skin freshener.)

Rock Sugar   Suck on it like a candy, use it to soothe your throat from a cough or cold, or add to tea and coffee.

look for a young hairy one. The top will come off easily with a knife; then punch out the three eyes.

In the vegetable section you will also find *glwar* (cluster beans), green peanuts, curry leaves from the kari plant, sour leaves for making chutneys, and knobs of fresh tumeric. Many of the stores import specialty vegetables from South India or Fiji. In the spring look for sweet custard apples, daruka asparagus, and prickly jackfruits.

You often have to ask at the front cash desk for the expensive specialty items. It takes thousands of dried crocus stigma to make 25 grams (one ounce) of saffron, which costs well over one hundred dollars, but the glorious fragrance and color it gives to food are worth it. A small one gram packet costs about four dollars.

Many dishes are decorated with pieces of silver leaf called *varak*. Varak comes in small sheets in a packet, separated by thin tissues. Don't try to handle the leaves with your hand. Lay the tissue over the dish and then peel it away. The leaf is perfectly edible, and there are claims that it's good for the digestion. Whatever, varak is certainly impressive and not too expensive (less than two dollars) for a special occasion.

The grocery store is also the place to buy Indian cookware. The *kadai* (or *karhai*), shaped like a wok, is the best investment you can make. Sizes range from regular to huge (about a meter [3 feet] across). The biggest ones are used on outside grills for family parties. The flat-bottomed round pans are used for making dough, and the three-footed round wooden board is for rolling roti. The metal dosa plate is designed for making paratha-type pancakes. Some of the heavy stone mortar and pestle sets called *dori kunda* or *chathu watta* are quite beautiful, even if you don't want to grind your spices by hand.

For the table itself, virtually everything, from tumblers to roti warmers, is stainless steel. This is not everyday ware—most Indian families use standard western crockery—but it is used for special occasions. Pieces are often engraved and given as gifts. Traditional meals are served on a *thali*—a metal dinner plate with a flat or curved rim holding several *katoris*, small bowls filled with the evening's dishes.

Sweet Shops

Traditionally, sweets are for eating at home, and they are also used for gifts. At holiday times everyone gives and receives these colorful

Bombay Sweets, at 6545 main st.

confections, and the lineups outside the stores often go around the block.

At **Bombay Sweets**, in the Punjabi Market, they will always let you try before you buy. One of the Shukla brothers will probably suggest you start with a pretzel-shaped, honey-filled, bright orange *jalebi*. Next, try one of the diamond-shaped pieces of *burfee* (much better tasting than their inelegant name would suggest). They come in a rainbow of pastel colors, often topped with pieces of silver varak; the green is pistachio, the pink is coconut and has a strawberry taste, and the gold ones are *besan* burfees made of almonds and rose butter. My own favorite is moist carrot burfee. Burfees are sweet but not loaded with sugar. A lot of the sweetness comes from the most important ingredient, milk, which is boiled down (often for hours) into a pasty substance with a yogurtlike consistency called *khoya*.

For nibbling, you can find roasted peanuts or fried chick peas. Light *matthi* wafers flavored with cumin seeds go well with drinks. I also like *ghatia* (they look like corn chips) made of gram flour and cumin seeds, and I am addicted to spicy *sao* or *samians,* little broken noodles that are made in a special grinder called a *moulsao* machine. A loose dough of gram or pea flour, salt, pepper, and cumin seed is mixed with water, turned through one of three changeable plates in the grinder, and then dropped into hot oil.

Bombay Sweets has expanded its shop, so you can now sit down and eat your treats right on the spot. The India Palace restaurant has a line of fancier and sometimes fresher sweets, which you can purchase at the front counter. At festival times, **Pabla's Exotic Foods**, which shares premises with the Himalaya Restaurant, arranges its sweets in a veritable mountain in the middle of the shop.

Sarees, Shilvar Kamis, and Sandals

By and large this section is for women only. Except for the turbans worn by Sikhs, Indian men have gone completely western. But the women have stayed with their traditional *sarees* and *shilvar kamis* trouser outfits. I did wonder at first if they would be offended by a western woman wearing an Indian costume. On the contrary, every lady I asked said she would be honored.

The saree is probably the most feminine costume in the world. Traditionally, it is a southern Hindu garment, but it is now worn, and

Saree at Ashoka's, 6621 main Street

FABRICS AND SAREES

At Ashoka's or any of the other dozen or so fabric shops
in the Punjabi market, you can buy sarees for as little as
twenty dollars. The shops also carry lengths for shilvar
kamis trouser suits as well as fine silks and chiffons.

loved, all over India. The graceful line and elegance of the draped saree gives a woman height and dignity. Sarees are bought in one piece, 110 centimeters (forty-five inches) across and 5.5 or 6.4 meters (six or seven yards) long. The drawstring cotton petticoat and midriff-baring choli top are bought separately. One size of saree fits all; the trick is in the wrapping, which, with a little practice, is easy to master.

Saree materials are gorgeous. At **Kejas Trading** (6642 Main) you can relax in the salon section while Kesar Shaliwal spreads out hand-embroidered chiffons and glittering gold-threaded silks in vivid royal colors from Benares. And at **Raj Trading** (6682 Main), Mr. Bhahan will go into his glass cases to show you the beautiful patterns of red wedding sarees. The less expensive polyester saree lengths at places like **Frontier Cloth** (6695 Main) are also attractive, with their bright, bold border patterns. Some of the fabrics come from India, but the bulk are from Japan, where the prints are made especially for the Indian market. Ashok Sharma, owner of **Ashoka Fabrics** (6621 Main) even had his supplier copy designs from popular Hindi film costumes.

The Punjabi-style *shilvar kamis,* with its long top and loose trousers, is also very comfortable. The matching scarf, called a *dupatte,* is of lighter material and, for Sikh women, doubles as a headcovering, especially at temple services. Shilvar kamis are also sold in lengths, 110 centimeters (forty-five inches) wide like sarees, but they are only 3.6 meters (four yards) in length. Some places, like the **Bargain Center** (6610 Main), specialize solely in these shilvar karmis pieces, which are always referred to as "suiting lengths". Often there is a cutting line on the fabric so that you can have a special design on the bodice or fancy sleeve borders.

If you don't sew yourself, all of the shops will give you the name of a nearby tailor who will make up shilvar kamis, to your specifications, at a very reasonable price. If you want to westernize the design a bit, ask for longer sleeves or tighter pants. Many younger women like the *churidar pajama* design. The trousers are cut on the bias, *jodhpur* style, and the bottom of the leg is bunched tightly like a set of bangles. In fact, *churidar* translates as "banglelike," and *pajamas* is originally an Indian word.

Most of the saree stores also stock imitation jewelry, glass bangles, and long, gold-colored earrings. The small colored dot that Indian women place in the middle of their forehead, slightly above the eyebrow

105

HOW TO WRAP A SAREE

1

Choli top and matching draw-string petticoat.

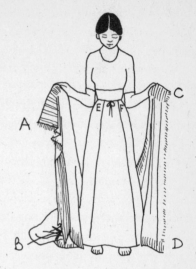

2

Tuck in C at point E.

3

Tuck in around waist. Turn around at point F.

4

Tuck in at back and around side until you reach point E again. Keep turning.

more . . .

line, is called a *bindi*. It can be painted on, but many shops carry ready-made dots with a light adhesive backing. *Kajal* is black eye paint in paste form. Powdered, it's called *surma*. Small pots of *sundur* are a special hair coloring for marriage ceremonies, and the big glass stones with the whisklike fans are for men's wedding turbans. The fancy braids are for bordering sarees, and you must purchase the whole roll.

Despite the large number of saree stores in the Punjabi Market, they all seem to have a different selection, and veterans say you must visit all of them before making your decision. Shan sarees has been there the longest, but I also like **East West** (6655 Main), with twelve years of service in Vancouver. The **Guru Bazaars** (6529 and 6660 Main) are branching out into western clothes, and **Flying Fashions** (6635 Main) sometimes has ready-made churidar pajamas on the rack.

One of the most interesting newcomers to the area is the **Shingar Emporium** (6522 Main), which specializes in imported footwear from India. The flat leather sandals are called *kolapuri*, and the curved slippers for men are called *jaipuri*.

Jewelry

If the gold-colored trinkets in the saree stores have given you a taste for the real thing, you might want to visit the jewelry stores in the Punjabi Market. The fanciest is **Bhindi Makanji** (or simply B.M.), at 6644 Main, and the presence of this store is a sign of the upgrading of the whole area. Headquartered in Fiji, this is their second store in Vancouver (the other is in the Granville Mall). B.M. deals exclusively in 22-carat gold. Pieces can be made to order right on the premises, and prices fluctuate daily with the changing market value of gold.

Western-style earrings and bracelets might seem conservative when compared to some of the Indian specialties like the elaborate *kandroos* (gold girdles) that are worn resting on one hip with a saree. For weddings, there is the *poncha* (five-finger rings attached to a gold bracelet). Nose pins, which also come clip-on style, armlets, silver *jhangars* (ankle bracelets laden with tiny bells), and toe rings are for everyday wear. A woman's jewelry is part of her dowry, and she wears it often and with pride; it represents her wealth and prestige.

If prices at B.M. seem a bit high, **Bharti Art Jewelry** (6604 Main) is more affordable. Although the owner, Bharti Parkh, carries some fine

107

Bring free A B end of saree around shoulders and adjust from fingertip to fingertip.

Tuck in G at F.

Pleat A B side of saree.

Drape A B over left shoulder.

filigreed silver pieces, she deals mainly in high-quality imitations. A necklace, earring, and ring set can run from ten dollars to thirty dollars.

Music and Video

The Indian film industry is gigantic, and billions of feet of celluloid are shot every year at studios all over the country. Don't expect too many art films or documentaries. Most of the movies are more like musical soap operas. The production values are not high, but these flicks are energetic and lots of fun. Just as fascinating are the antics of all the stars, which you can read about in one of the English-language fan magazines.

If you want to take in an Indian movie the **York** (639 Commercial) shows Hindi films, which are usually subtitled in English. If you have a video playback machine, you can rent movies. Cassettes are released simultaneously with the film, and shops like Mann's video in the Punjabi Market are booming.

The scores from popular films are also in great demand. The songs are almost always dubbed, and famous film singers like Kishor Kumar can do as much for box offices as the name of the male hero. For classical music, Ravi Shankar is still the top instrumentalist, but have you heard Ali Agah Khan? For classical songs, Mahdi Hassan is one of the top recording artists.

The local community is large enough now to bring many of the top performing artists to Vancouver on tour. For information, watch the local newspapers, or look for posters in the Main Street area stores.

Festivals and Holidays

The most important festival for Sikhs is *Baisahki* in early April. Although Baisahki is celebrated throughout India as the spring festival, for Sikhs, this was the day in 1699 when the tenth master, Guru Gobind Singh, rose up against the Muslims and declared the birth of the *Khalsa* brotherhood.

This day, which marks the beginning of the Sikh nation, is celebrated in grand fashion with a colorful procession of floats and bands, followed by thousands of men, women, and children. It starts at the Ross Street Temple and winds its way up Main Street to the market area. The focus of the parade is the magnificently draped vehicle

109

9   10

Gather remaining portion of saree and make 4-5″ (10-13 cm) pleats.

Tuck in at waist.

carrying the Sikh holy book. At the height of the festivities, a helicopter flies overhead and showers the huge crowds with flower petals. The celebration continues all day in the market with Punjabi folk songs and the traditional *bhangra* dance. All the shops are open and Baisahki is always marked by special sales events.

Divali is the major fall festival. All the shops are decorated with lights, and the sweet shops are full of special treats. Like Baisahki, Divali is celebrated by all religious groups, but its special significance is for Hindus. Coming at the end of October or early November, it usually lasts four days and marks the beginning of the new year.

There are several Hindu legends associated with Divali, but the most common one is the return of Lord Ram from the jungle after a fourteen-year exile ordered by his mother. Also called the Festival of Lights, this holiday welcomes him back into the everyday world, with much rejoicing, including lots of firecrackers and gifts of sweets to friends and relatives. Divali is a family festival celebrated mostly at home, but the Hindu Temple does sponsor a special cultural evening at one of the large downtown theaters. This is an opportunity to see many of the unique classical Indian dances, like the *bharata-natyam*, a story or lyric poem set to music and interpreted by intricate hand and eye movements.

The most important event in the lunar Muslim calendar is *Ramadan*. Usually coinciding with August, it is a period of self-control involving fasting and other demonstrations of self-restraint. At the end of Ramadan, there is a large celebration called the *Eid-al-Fitr*.

August 14 is the anniversary of the creation of Pakistan in 1947. This is a day of special festivities to which the public is invited. For information about dates or places, call the *imam* (prayer leader) of Greater Vancouver at 270-3052.

Around Town

Since the consolidation of the Punjabi Market area on Main Street is relatively recent, many of the best Indian restaurants and stores are scattered around town. Here are some recommendations.

The **India Gate** at Robson and Seymour is one of the best places to eat on Theater Row. It's patronized at noon by many Indian business-men and gets one of the top ratings for Indian food in the whole city.

The Raga is the newest, fanciest and probably now the best Indian

111

TO MAKE PURIS

You will need: 500 ml (2 cups) whole wheat flour
                     45 ml (3 tbsps) ghee
                     125 to 250 ml (½ to 1 cup) lukewarm
                     water

Combine the flour and ghee with your fingers until it has the consistency of coarse meal. Add the water gradually, blending and stirring until the dough can be made into a firm ball.

Knead the dough for seven to eight minutes.

To make each puri, break off a small piece of dough about 2.5 cm (1 inch) in diameter and roll it in your hands to slightly flatten the ball. Flour the puri ball and your woking surface. Roll out the ball until it is wafer thin, just less than 3mm (⅛ in) thick.

Deep fry the puris in moderately hot oil. Spoon the oil over them as they fry.

restaurant in Vancouver. The chicken and naan bread that comes from Raga's authentic tandoor clay oven gets at least five stars.

For a sampling of Fijian-style Indian food, try **Sanjay's** (1344 Lonsdale) in North Vancouver. Try the *eka-vaka-lolo,* trout or red snapper steamed in coconut milk. In Gastown, the **Kilimanjaro** (308 Water Street) specializes in East African dishes like *piri-piri.* Very hot peppers are simmered, usually in lemon juice, then served over prawns or chicken.

For an inexpensive way to sample Indian food, the **South Vancouver Neighborhood House** at 49th and Victoria has an Indian lunch the first Thursday of every month, for three dollars per person. The House also sponsors **Sami's Samosas**, a new business that distributes foods made by Indian housewives. You can buy their products at the Neighborhood House.

My personal favorite of all the Indian restaurants in Vancouver is the **Ashiana** (5076 Victoria Drive). This is a new place, and I have my fingers crossed for its future. The menu is all a la carte and the dishes are small and inexpensive enough that you can sample two or three. The desserts here come fresh from the excellent sweet shop adjoining, and their milky *rasjoullah* tastes of heaven. This part of Victoria Drive also has a little cluster of Indian shops, including the brand new premises of **Ambika Foods** (5125 Victoria) and the spacious quarters of the **India Sari Palace** at 33rd and Victoria.

The **Calabria Meat Market** (5223 Victoria) supplies goat meat for Indian cooks. Muslims buy their mutton at one of the two **Halal** meat stores (10th and Fraser and 25th and Main). All the meats here are prepared according to the ritual practices of Islam.

Special mention must be made of **Patel's** (2210 Commercial), the first and the largest of the Indian foodstores. This is truly a "super" market, where you can find everything from freshly made chapatis to imported Indian dental cream. People come from all over the Pacific Northwest for their wide selection of regional specialties, plus their up-to-date stock of record albums and video cassettes of the latest films. The service is excellent, and this is one place where you can feel comfortable asking lots of questions.

The **Hindu Temple** is a simple stucco building at 3885 Albert Street in Burnaby. Inside the main prayer hall you'll find exquisite waxen images of Lord Krishna and his wife Radda on the front stage area.

113

Remove your shoes when you enter, and put them to one side of the door. Women and men sit on separate sides of the temple, with ladies on the right. The Sunday service starts at 10:30 A.M. and continues for two hours. Although the songs, prayers, and talks are in Hindi, there is often an English-speaking guest who gives a talk on Sunday mornings.

If you want to learn one of the Indian languages, the Ross Street Sikh Temple offers classes in Punjabi for children and adults. At the Hindu Temple you can learn Hindi, Gujarati, or Sanskrit.

The Burnaby Temple also has classes in yoga and, if there's a demand for it, Indian classical dancing. For year-round lessons, the Natraj School of Dancing is located in North Vancouver. Telephone: 988-9774.

If You Want to Know More

Half a dozen newspapers are published for the local Indian community, usually biweekly, and several of them are in English. You can usually pick up a copy in one of the local Indian stores, but annual subscriptions are also available. According to a recent independent survey, *The Link* (PO Box 76873, Station S V5R 5T3) is the most widely read of these papers and does seem to have the best coverage of local news. Ujjal Dosanjh's political columns pull no punches, and editor Promod Puri's *What's Happening* items are a good way to keep in touch with upcoming events.

And finally, for an all-round directory of retail and wholesale businesses, cultural organizations, and restaurants, try the *Trade and Cultural Directory: Indo Canadians in the 1980s,* published at 545 East Broadway.

Although the first Sikhs arrived at the turn of the century, the real growth of the community has been in the last ten years. Today, after London, England, Vancouver has the largest Indian immigrant population in the world. But as yet, the neighborhood around 49th and Main is virtually undiscovered as an area for finding Indian food, restaurants, and gifts. So get out and start exploring.

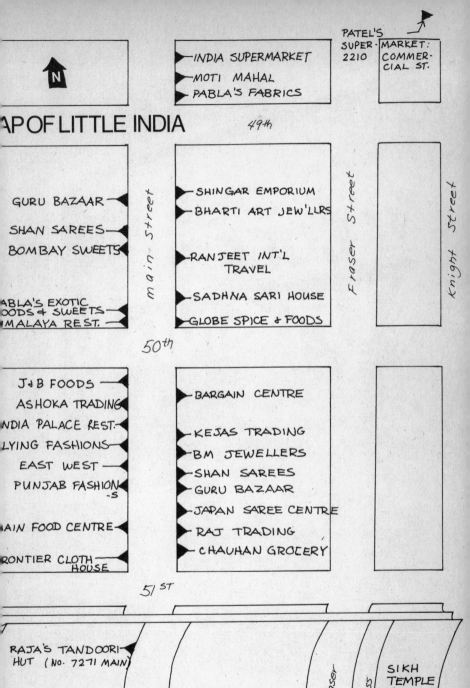

MAP OF LITTLE INDIA

N

INDIA SUPERMARKET
MOTI MAHAL
PABLA'S FABRICS

PATEL'S SUPER-2210

MARKET: COMMERCIAL ST.

49th

main street

Fraser Street

Knight Street

GURU BAZAAR

SHAN SAREES

BOMBAY SWEETS

PABLA'S EXOTIC
FOODS & SWEETS

MALAYA REST.

SHINGAR EMPORIUM

BHARTI ART JEW'LLRS

RANJEET INT'L TRAVEL

SADHNA SARI HOUSE

GLOBE SPICE & FOODS

50th

J & B FOODS

ASHOKA TRADING

INDIA PALACE REST.

FLYING FASHIONS

EAST WEST

PUNJAB FASHIONS

MAIN FOOD CENTRE

FRONTIER CLOTH HOUSE

BARGAIN CENTRE

KEJAS TRADING

BM JEWELLERS

SHAN SAREES

GURU BAZAAR

JAPAN SAREE CENTRE

RAJ TRADING

CHAUHAN GROCERY

51 ST

RAJA'S TANDOORI HUT (NO. 7271 MAIN)

Fraser

Ross

SIKH TEMPLE

S. W. Marine Drive

115

'Athenian' grocery & coffee shop at 3143 W. Broadway

GREEKTOWN

On its best summer days when the sand is hot, the water warm, and the sky gets that clear Aegean blue color, Vancouver could be a little bit of Greece. To further the illusion, wander down to West Broadway where it meets MacDonald, and you're in Greektown. For half a dozen blocks most of the businesses are Greek owned and operated, and the national colors of blue and white are everywhere. The names of the shops and stores—Minerva, Poseidon, Parthenon, Marathon, Acropol— are a virtual roll call of classical history and mythology. Here you can shop for the latest record albums, hand pick the best olives in town, invest in an evil eye to ward off danger, or just sit under the shade trees with a cup of thick, sweet coffee and leaf through the latest magazine from Athens.

Visiting Greektown and St. George's Church

Although Greeks are scattered all over the city, the West Broadway area has the strongest residential component as well as being the center for commercial activity. The Greek shops and restaurants actually start as far east as Fir Street and continue right down to Alma, but the strongest concentration is the area where MacDonald and Broadway intersect. There's also a small cluster of Greek restaurants and stores over on 4th Avenue—more or less the northern border of Greektown.

From Greektown it is not far to St. George's Orthodox Church at 31st and Arbutus. Although there are still strong feelings that the Church should have been located in Greektown, it is the pride of the Greek community and all are invited to visit. In fact, the Church has published a little guide booklet called *A Personal Welcome* that takes you on an artistic, architectural, and religious tour of the Church. The only request to visitors is that women not wear pants or shorts.

If you do attend one of the Sunday services, go up the side aisles of the church, not through the main gates, which face the altar. If you wish,

THE GREEK ORTHODOX CHURCH

An antique censer for burning incense during church services.

Although Greeks have assimilated easily into North American culture, they have retained a strong Greek identity, largely due to the influences of the Greek Orthodox Church. When Greece was a subject state of the Ottoman Empire, it was the Greek Church, working underground and in secret, that kept alive the Greek language and culture. Though the circumstances have changed today, the Church remains the focus of a great deal of community activity in the Vancouver area.

purchase a candle at the door and light it; regular worshipers then make a small prayer and kiss the icons. The service is usually in Greek, and the rich environment of royal blues, gold, and white combined with the sweet smell of incense and the hypnotic rhythm of Byzantine chanting will all have their effect, creating a feeling of peace.

The icons are one of the most interesting features of the Eastern Church. These pictures of Christ, or one of the saints, are revered as "windowframes" where worshipers can "see" these holy human beings.

Greek Food

Greek cuisine is a wonderful mixture of influences, partly because Greece was the crossroads for eastern and western trade, partly because it was occupied by foreign invaders for so much of its history. Eggplants, lemons, and rice came from India. Honey-filled baclava was a Turkish favorite, and the thin filo pastry originated from Persia. The Ottoman Turks, who occupied Greece for four hundred years, had the strongest effect on Greek cooking. *Moussaka* and yogurt came from these rulers as did their special way of preparing coffee. When the Venetians took over Greece in the 1700s, they introduced macaroni and tomato-based sauces.

One of the best things about Greek restaurants are the *orektika* or more commonly, *mezethes* (*mezes* for short). They are similar to French hor d'oevres or North American appetizers but far more imaginative and not limited to before dinner eating. Mezes are eaten from midafternoon until late in the evening, and the choice is endless, from a few squares of cheese, some pistachio nuts, and cold beans to tiny meals—*kalamari* (deep-fried squid), *sikotakia* (sauteed chicken livers), or bits of broiled meats. Some of the most familiar Greek foods fall into the mezes category—*tiropitta* and *spanakopitta* (squares or triangles of cheese and spinach pie), *keftedes* (meatballs), *taramosalata* (puréed carp roe), and *dolmathes* (grape leaves stuffed with rice and ground meat).

In North America a *horiatiki* (Greek village salad) is made up of olives, cucumber, onions, tomato, green pepper, and crumbled *feta* cheese. In a Greek village the daily salad would be done a little differently. There, lettuce is the main ingredient—romaine, chicory, endive, and iceberg—and never torn, but finely sliced. The vegetables depend solely on what's fresh; anything from green peas to string beans

119

TIROPITTAS (CHEESE PIES)

These cheese-filled triangles can be made in any size for appetizers or main courses. Making them is time-consuming, but relaxing, and the results are definitely impressive.

You will need: 250 gm (½ lb) feta cheese
200 ml (¾ cup) baking cheese
50 ml (¼ cup) finely chopped fresh parsley
3 medium eggs, well beaten
250 gm (½ lb) unsalted butter melted
250 gm (½ lb) filo at room temperature

Rinse feta and crumble into a bowl. Add baking cheese and parsley. Mix. Add beaten eggs. Mix until well blended.

Cut filo sheets into long strips about 3 inches (10 cm) wide for small appetizers.

Take a single sheet and brush with melted butter. Fold each side toward the center and brush again. Place a small spoonful of the cheese mixture in the center about 3 cm (1 inch) from the end. Fold one corner over to form a triangle. Continue folding (and brushing with butter) from side to side in neat triangles to end of filo strip. Trim.

Place triangles on an ungreased cookie sheet. Brush with butter. Bake at 190° C (375° F) for 15 to 20 minutes until golden brown. Serve warm.

can be included. The cheese is usually in a separate dish and added for personal taste. In fact, for an authentic Greek meal, all the dishes are served at once, so the women can enjoy eating along with everyone else, instead of getting up to replenish the table.

Greek soups are, unfortunately, not very well known here. Hearty navy-bean *fassoulada*—the national dish of Greece—is a meal in itself. *Avgolemeno,* a chicken-broth-based soup with egg (*avego*) and blended with a little lemon juice (*lemeno*), is a light, delicate soup and, when thickened, is the most popular of the Greek sauces. The Greeks also claim credit for inventing bouillabaisse, which they say they taught to the cooks of southern France when the area round Marseille was a colony in the fourth and fifth centuries B.C. The Greek fish soup, *kaccavia,* was named after the pot in which Greek fishermen simmered their assortment of freshly caught fish.

Greece is surrounded by water, and *psari* (fish) is a major source of food. Whole fish are pan-fried (*tiganita*) in hot oil until the outside is crusty. *Plaki* (fillets) are baked with tomato sauces or wrapped in paper to keep in the moisture. Tiny pieces of kalamari or *oktapodi* (octopus) can be marinated and eaten cold or quickly deep-fried. If you chance upon *achinoi* (sea urchin), try it raw on the half-shell with a squeeze of lemon.

Greece may have a rich aquatic environment, but the land itself is poor; the soil is rocky and barren, the terrain rugged with little grazing land. That's why you don't find much beef, although veal is very popular, in Greek cooking—only goats and sheep can really survive. It's from these two animals, particularly *arni* (lamb), that the succulent Greek dishes come. Leg of lamb is often rubbed with olive oil and fresh oregano and basted with a tomato sauce while it is oven roasted for several hours. For *souvlaki,* lamb is cut into chunks, threaded on a skewer, and roasted over charcoal.

Ground lamb goes a lot further when it is layered with sliced eggplant and covered with a thick white béchamel sauce for moussaka. *Pasticio* (macaroni combined with ground beef or lamb) is a casserole dish and a special favorite with children. And then there are the countless rice *pilafs* made with vegetables or seafood.

To please Canadian tastes, there is always a dessert menu in the local Greek restaurants. Flaky squares of *baclava* saturated with honey and filled with nuts are most famous, but it's just the beginning of a

GREEK SNACKS AND SWEETS

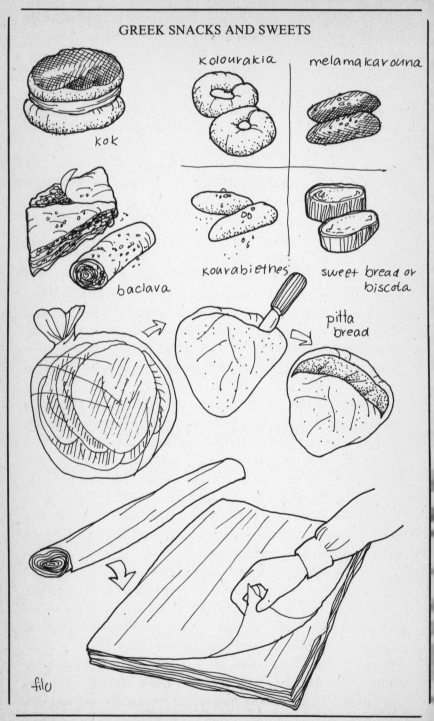

kok

Kolourakia

melamakarouna

baclava

kourabiethes

sweet bread or biscota

pitta bread

filo

sweet list that can include shortbread cookies, cheese cakes, pastry puffs filled with rich creams and custards, and delicious fruit preserves.

Greek coffee finishes a meal and should be served with a glass of cold water to cut the sweetness and wash away the coffee grounds. Sugar is added while the coffee is being made, so in a restaurant you must order it *sketo* (plain), *metrio* (medium sweet), or *vari glyko* (very sweet).

After coffee, Metaxa brandy is reputed to be one of the finest brandy liquers in the world and, along with *retsina* and *ouzo*, is available at local liquor stores. A lot of non-Greeks dislike the strong pine flavor of retsina, but it's worth a try. For an interesting champagne-type drink, mix it with soda or mineral water. Ouzo, with its strong anise taste, is properly an aperitif. Greeks sometimes drink in neat, but more often on ice. You can also add tepid water, which turns the clear liquid cloudy.

One important point: in Greece ouzo is never drunk alone. Whenever you order an ouzo you also receive a meze. One can generalize and say that drinking always involves eating in Greek culture.

If you're drinking with a Greek, always let him refill your glass. When you want to make a toast, the word for good health and good cheer is "yasoo".

Greektown Restaurants

In most Greek restaurants the food has been adapted to Canadian tastes—less olive oil, larger portions, and a standardized menu that varies little with the seasons. However, the Greeks who own and run these restaurants also know their Canadian patrons expect Greek food and atmosphere, and, with a few variations and adaptations, that is what you get.

Vassilis Taverna (2883 West Broadway) consistently gets high ratings from local restaurant critics. Owner Andre Demiris used to be the proprietor of the Greek University Delicatessan at the same spot but a couple of years ago decided to go the restaurant route. His wife, Georgia, does the cooking—try her daily fassoulada soup—and the kids wait on tables. At lunchtime Vassilis is a meeting place for many of the local merchants and a favorite spot for visiting Greek sailors.

For many years, the **Acropol** (2946 West Broadway) was an old-

marathon Restaurant at 3121 W. Broadway.

style kitchen restaurant where the day's fare was laid out on steam tables. It's been recently modernized, but the old quality remains, and the Acropol has one of the most varied menus on the street. Their seafood platter with trout, crab, prawns, and roe is huge, and, for something unusual, try the *gyros*, ground beef with slices of lamb cooked on a spit.

If the Acropol has changed, a lot of it has to do with the phenomenal success of **Orestes** at 3116 West Broadway. In the summer of 1973 Aristides Pasparakis, a metallurgy PhD graduate from the University of British Columbia, created a simple whitewashed restaurant that had the feel of a Mediterranean taverna. His menu was traditional, but his style meshed perfectly with the tastes of young Canadians who wanted elegance and white wine with their ethnic food. Orestes is now under the management of Aristides' first partner, Blaine Culling. It's a popular meeting place—the unofficial Kitsilano community center—and lots of people drop by in the evening just to drink and snack in the downstairs bar.

The **Marathon** (3121 West Broadway) has been recommended to me many times as the most authentic Greek restaurant in the area. Sophia Glover and her son have their open kitchen just inside the door, and you can check out the day's specialties at the nearby steam table. Sophia's personal recommendation is her lamb casserole. Cooked in tomato sauce on top of the stove, she starts it early in the morning, and by lunchtime it is perfect.

Athene's (3618 West Broadway) is a new restaurant and well worth trying. The interior is cool and relaxing, and the prices are reasonable. Their mixed platter for two is a good bargain, and, with a couple of glasses of wine, dinner for two can come in under twenty-five dollars.

Stavros (1619 West Broadway) is lots of fun and seems to get some of the best belly dancers for evening entertainment. A couple of blocks away, at 1967 West Broadway, **Aretousa** is the only Greek restaurant in town that specializes in food from the island of Crete. Try their spinach pie. Instead of flaky filo, the crust is a thicker pastry pinched around the edges like an Indian samosa.

Simpatico (2222 West 4th Avenue) has long had a reputation for its whole wheat pizza, but the Greek food is ample, delicious, and well priced. It's an excellent place if you've got the whole family to feed. At **Romio's Taverna** (2272 West 4th Avenue) try the *kalamarakia tiganita*

125

'Parthenon' at 2968 W. Broadway.

(marinated pan-fried tiny squid). You won't find squid done this way in many restaurants.

The Kaffenion: For Men Only

Greek men like to socialize together—that means without women. In Greektown they gather at places like **Broadway Billiards** (3205 West Broadway) and **Kitsilano Billiards** (3255 West Broadway), which are substitutes for the old-style *kaffenion* (coffee house) that was an essential part of every village. In a few of the restaurants a section of tables, usually near the front, are implicitly reserved for men where they can chat, gossip, and perhaps do some business. The **Athens Social Club** upstairs (3239 West Broadway) is a licensed gambling club and the largest kaffenion in Greektown.

Shopping in Greektown

Whether you want to replicate some of the famous dishes you've sampled in one of the restaurants or try your hand at some Greek-style home cooking, all of the ingredients are available along the Greek section of West Broadway where food is the focal point.

If you are gift shopping, you'll find lots of jewelry and other little trinkets, but your best finds may be in the food stores. An imported meze or a bottle of extra sweet preserves could be the "something different" you've been looking for.

Greek Foodstores

Angelo Cosiris opened the first Greek food store on Broadway in 1966. His son, Louis, now manages the **Parthenon** (2968 West Broadway) and stocks imported specialties from Greece, Turkey, India, Israel, Morocco, and all the Arabian countries, so don't be surprised to find matzo beside the pasta and falafel next to the filo.

The Parthenon is certainly the biggest food store on the street; in fact it has the largest selection of cheeses and cold meats in town. But the **Athenian** (3145 West Broadway) provides good competition, especially since the husband and wife Paskalidis team started to specialize in roasting their own coffees. The **Seven Seas** fish store (2344 West 4th Avenue) also has a good selection of imported Greek specialty items.

GREEK FOOD

Tiny Melitzanes   Eggplant stuffed with pimento makes a tasty treat.

Greek Shortening   It's ninety-nine percent olive oil and adds extra flavor if you're sautéeing meats, pork, or game. Mix it with regular cooking oil (thirty percent fytini, seventy percent regular oil).

Greek-Style Macaroni   These drinking-straw sized tubes are used for making pasticio.

Beans from Greece   Serve cold for a meze.

Oregano from Greece   The real thing. Often the oregano you get in super-markets is actually thyme-based.

Greek Chocolate   These bars are made Swiss style—very smooth with lots of milk.

A Shelf-By-Shelf Guide to a Greek Food Store

Whichever Greek food store you're shopping at, head first for the olives where you can scoop out as many as you want from the big, white plastic buckets.

There are several kinds of Greek olives. The long, oval-shaped, deep purple ones are called *kalamata,* after the city in the southern Peloponnesus Peninsula. There are two varieties of black olives commonly found in Vancouver: the small, wrinkled ones have the least meat of all but have a dry, salty flavor; the big, round ones are especially juicy but are often more brownish than black. They're occasionally called by their official name, Amphissian. Don't be put off if there's a moldy film covering the skin; that's the sign of a good brine. Finally, the big green olives are picked unripe and are the best choice if you like a slightly bitter edge.

The olive oil section always overwhelms me with dozens of Italian brands mixed in with the Greek. Greek oil is generally less refined and more flavorful than other European oils. The dark green virgin oil is the most expensive because it comes from the first pressing. Use sparingly as it can affect the flavor of a dish, but it is the best you can get for salads. Mix one part of good vegetable oil to two parts Greek olive oil for best results. There are lots of brands of good medium oil like Kalamata, Minerva, and Elai.

On the same shelf are cans of unique Greek shortening. Soft and yellow *fytini* is ninety-five percent olive oil. It's super for baking, and every Greek cook I've talked to recommends it heated up and mixed with rice or tossed with spaghetti. Top with dry, shredded mizithra cheese.

Two walls of the Parthenon are taken up with their wide selection of meats and cheese. Although it was the Greeks who gave the world its first salami, most of the meats are Italian or German. The exception is the Greek sausage called *loukanika.* Loukanika are made locally at **West Side Meats** (3431 West Broadway), but it's just as easy to get them in one of the groceries. These pork sausages are seasoned with sage and orange rind. Cut one up into small pieces, fry, and sprinkle with lemon juice—or better still, try them barbecued.

There are four Greek cheeses. Feta isn't just for salads; it's fine all on its own. There's not enough Greek feta for export, but sometimes the

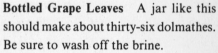

MORE GREEK FOOD

Bottled Grape Leaves   A jar like this should make about thirty-six dolmathes. Be sure to wash off the brine.

Mountain Tea   There's no cure for the common cold, but this sure helps a lot.

Canned Dolmathes   Eat cold as is with a little lemon. Not as good as home-made, but a close second.

Mastic   Used sometimes as a flavoring in cooking, or put a spoonful in cold water for a distinctive summer drink. Just nibble away at it while you sip the flavored water.

stores have the real goat's milk feta from Rumania or Quebec, and it's worth asking for, but more often you will find cow's milk feta made here in Canada. If you buy it wet from the barrel, put the cheese in your own salt solution at home, and it will stay fresh for months. Don't forget to rinse it off before eating.

Mizithra is made from the whey left over from feta. It is dry and mild and is used for baking, or try it on toast with a little olive oil and oregano. *Kefalotyri* is a hard, salty baking cheese. Cut the slices about 1 cm (half an inch) thick, dip in a light flour and egg batter, fry in hot oil on both sides for a few minutes, and then sprinkle with lemon juice, and you've got *saganaki,* my favorite meze. If you like your saganaki runny, use soft *kasseri,* a golden cheese that glistens with oil. This is also a fine cheese for everyday table use.

There are all kinds of canned and bottled specialties that you can add to your plates of ready-made mezethes. Tinned dolmathes should be served cold with yogurt or a sprinkle of lemon juice. Eat hot green *salonika* peppers (usually called by their Italian name *pepperonchini*) alone or put them in a salad. The pickled *volvi* (pink onions) are uniquely Greek, as are tiny stuffed eggplants. Their sour taste is offset by the smooth olive oil marinade. *Tursi anakatemeno* (pickled vegetables) can be bought bottled or by the gram. Add a little olive oil, oregano, mint, or even chili peppers to make the brine more interesting.

Although it comes in large tins, Greek tomato paste is worth trying. It is much sweeter and has a better color than Italian brands, and, if you cover the open tin with a little olive oil, it will keep for months in the fridge.

In the dried foods section, there are dozens of different beans; the big, broad fava ones are the most popular for soups. Dried chick peas, salted or unsalted, and pumpkin seeds are for snacking.

If you are planning on any Greek baking, dark Greek sultana raisins are especially sweet, and you might know Corinthian raisins as currants. White ammonia powder is a leavening agent that gives Greek cookies their airy lightness, and packaged Yiotis custard powder is a fast and popular dessert.

There are always a couple of rows of bottled preserves—sour cherry, bitter oranges, grape, quince, and even eggplant. Don't confuse them with jams. These are Greek spoon desserts. A small amount is served on a plate with a glass of cold water on the side to cut the sugar.

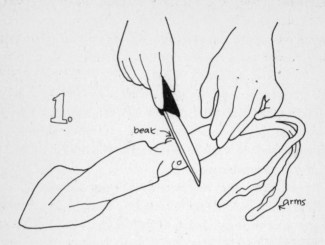

Cut through the arms near the eyes. With thumb and forefinger feel for and remove the inedible beak located near the cut.

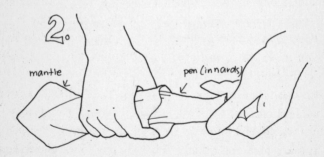

Feel inside mantle and remove innards. (This can be done under cold water which makes it easier to loosen the 'pen'.)

On the same shelf, in similar sized bottles, you'll find *mastic* or *mastiha,* a gummy, white licorice-flavored sweet that comes from the mastic tree. Put a spoonful in a tall, cold glass of water and sip it through a hot summer afternoon.

Greek *meli* (honey) is highly perfumed, very thick, and very, very sweet. In fact, many connoisseurs claim this is the best honey in the world. If you can forget about calories, ask for a piece of chocolate or vanilla halvah. This confection is nothing but pure sugar and lots of butter, but it is a wonderful treat.

Mint, dill, bay leaf, marjoram, coriander, and basil (a pot in the window means welcome) are among the most common Greek herbs. Imported Greek oregano is much stronger than the North American variety, and you can buy it in dried bunches. *Fascomelo* (sage) and camomile come to Canada the same way and are often used to brew up excellent teas. The former is reputed to be good for congestion, and camomile is recommended for stomach upsets and a good night's sleep, especially for children.

Greek coffee is ground very fine, and Papagalos (with the distinctive green parrot on the package), Brava, and Brazita are the most famous brands. For the best coffee, get it ground at the Athenian Grocery where Anastasios Paskalidis has invented his own machines (which he also wholesales) for roasting and grinding beans to any specification. The Athenian stocks all kinds of coffee, but, for Greek style, ask for the house brand, Helexia or Venizelos, named in honor of Greece's beloved modern statesman.

Fish

The old Poseidon Fish Store next to the Parthenon has been renamed the Broadway Fish Market. But the new owners still carry lots of Greek specialties, like fresh skate (just pan-fry in butter) or perch (great barbecued whole). Greek cooks love to cook from scratch, and the window of Broadway is full of whole, uncleaned fish. And they have fish heads; red snapper is great for soup stock. Of course you will find lots of squid, cuttlefish, and octopus.

In the cooler there is a pail of *lakerda* (salted and marinated tuna). Squeeze the requisite half lemon over a small piece, and have it cold. The pieces of *bacaliaro* (dried cod) need to be soaked overnight (change the water at least twice!) before lightly frying or baking them. Salted

133

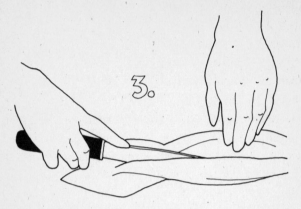

Cut the mantle open from top to tail on one side only so it can be washed inside and out.

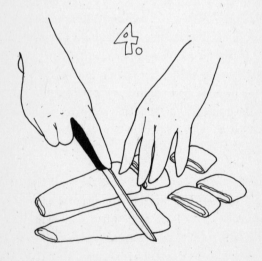

Then cut it into bite-sized pieces.

Sprinkle *kalamari* pieces with lemon juice, dip in a mixture of one beaten egg and 25 ml (2 tbsp) milk, roll in flour and deep fry until lightly browned.

anchovies come by the gram from one of the big twenty-five kilogram tins, and the jars of reddish orange fish eggs are mullet roe. Pureed with olive oil and white bread, they are transformed into the *taramosalata* you find on every mezethes list.

Broadway's top competition is the **Seven Seas** (ft. Lonsdale N. Van.). The Falcos have their own boats, and a big part of their trade is wholesale. The grocery section is bigger than Broadway's with a good variety of cheeses, oil, coffee, and many canned and bottled imported goods. Most of the fish is filleted here, and you will find all the Greek favorites in their freezer section—sardines, smelts, stickleback, mullet, and bream. The mullet is from Greece; it is bony but very tasty when it's pan-fried or broiled with olive oil and lemon sauce. Tiny bream are a bargain at just over two dollars a kilogram. They make an excellent stock.

Breads and Sweets

Broadway Bakery and Pastry (3155 West Broadway) has been serving the local community for over twenty years. This is the place for fresh *pitta,* the flat, oval-shaped bread that can be cut open and filled with everything from souvlaki to salad to hamburger. Greek loaf bread is usually big and round, and very airy.

As for the sweets, don't stop with baclava. There is also honey-filled *melomakarouna,* rolled in finely chopped walnuts. *Kourabiethes* have the same oval shape, but they are more like shortbreads, dusted with fine white confectioner's sugar. Another shortbread-like cookie, *koulourakia,* comes in a variety of different shapes. Koulourakia were originally an Easter specialty, though now they are sold year-round.

It's hard to sip on a cup of Greek coffee without a sweet *pasta* (not to be confused with Italian noodles), and Broadway's variety of cream-filled delights fill the bill. I particularly like the chocolate sandwich one called *kok.*

If you are making your own baclava or spanokopitta, Broadway Bakery stocks filo, but ironically it is made by the other famous local Greek baker, Louis Zerbino. Louis sold his old bakery at 2320 West 4th Avenue to a Chinese family who continue to sell Greek pastry, including ready-made cheese and spinach pies. After a trip abroad, Louis is back in Vancouver. He doesn't have a new bakery yet, but he is making hand-rolled filo again and selling it to local stores like Broadway Bakery and **Pascal's** (4526 West 10th Avenue).

GREEK GIFTS

Metal Briki Select the heaviest one you can find for making authentic Greek coffee.

Koboloi or Worry Beads Fiddle with them enough, and it takes your mind off your troubles.

A Greek Calendar Tear off a day at a time. On the back of each page is a poem, recipe, or limerick.

Greek Sailors' Hats These classic navy blue wool peaked caps make great gifts.

From Children's Wear to Bouzouki Music: Gift Shopping in Greektown

You can start your gift shopping on the east side of MacDonald at **Vicky's Children's Wear** (2680 West Broadway). Owner John Feretos keeps a good stock of hand embroidered and crocheted baby clothes imported from Greece at prices ranging from ten to fifty dollars. For special occasions, Mr. Feretos also designs fancy dresses and capes. Vicky's also has a good selection of Greek linens.

If you fancy some Mediterranean-style jewelry, **Edward Tokatlian Creative Jewellers** (2819 West Broadway) is the place to go. Edward and his wife, Rosie, are Armenians, although they come from Greece, and they've had this store for eleven years. If you want to see something fancy, ask to see their delicately filigreed gold rings. The small turquoise balls with black centers are evil eyes, which many Greeks wear around their necks. An evil eye with a band of 14-carat gold costs around twenty dollars. In fact, anything turquoise wards off evil, and the flat, gold pendants with tiny turquoise stones are presented as good luck talismans to newborn babies.

Minerva Greek Imports (2856 West Broadway) has a hodge-podge of religious icons, children's clothes, hand-painted plates, wooden wine gourds, and authentic Greek woolen sailor's caps. Just inside the door is all the wedding and baptismal paraphernalia. The huge candles draped with netting, called *lambathes,* come in twos and are carried in the wedding procession by children or bridesmaids. Every guest at a wedding or baptism receives a little *boubonniere,* a smaller piece of netting twisted around five or seven small, eye-shaped almond candies.

If you want to make your own Greek coffee, Minerva is the place to find a long-handled *briki.* They cost between three and five dollars, and you can use one for years. And to properly appreciate Greek coffee, invest in the tiny demitasse cups on the same shelf.

The best part of Minerva is at the back where all the record albums and tapes are located. Most of the titles are written in Greek script, so ask for help from owner Nike Georgiopoulos, who will be happy to tell you about the latest songs and the most popular singers.

There are many kinds of Greek music to choose from—bouzouki instrumentals, folkdance music, or the political songs of Theodorakis, who was imprisoned during the reign of the military junta in the early

THE BEST OF GREEK MUSIC

Mariza Koh   Probably the most popular female vocalist in Greece today.

Niko Xylouris   The recent death of this most beloved Cretian folk singer was mourned all over the country.

Prodomus Tasaousakis   One of the greats from the rebetika era, which was biggest in Greece in the 1920s and 1930s.

seventies. And there's *rebetika,* the underground street music that grew up in the twenties and thirties, when people would gather at the kaffenia, play the bouzouki, and sing their own ballads of love and defiance. Vasilis Tsitsanis and George M. Mitsakis were two of the most famous rebetika singers. Mariza Koh is one of the most progressive modern singers of Greek popular songs, and she sometimes performs in Vancouver.

Getting There is Half the Fun: Greek Travel Agencies

If all this Greek music starts you dreaming of the real thing, stop in at **Omega Travel** (2932 West Broadway), one of the three Greek agencies in the area. They all offer cheap charter flights, which are also available to non-Greeks.

The tiny Omega office gets so crowded at times it seems to double as a local social club. Perhaps that's because owner Nick Panos is one of the most involved people in the local community. Andry and Andros Sofocleous, at **Athenon Travel** (3271 West Broadway), are also Greek radio personalities. They have their own recording studios, and Mrs. Sofocleous' weekly program of the latest Greek music can be heard every Sunday afternoon on CJJC radio (800 on the A.M. dial). Mike Georgiopoulos, the owner of Minerva, follows with his show every Sunday from four to seven p.m.

Crown Travel Service at 2289 West Broadway doubles as the Athenium College. In the back room you can see a full-sized classroom where owner and teacher George Boutsakis instructs local youngsters in Greek language and writing after their regular school day is finished.

Night Life

The **Symposion Restaurant and Cabaret** (2291 West Broadway) has had a series of owners who come and go with mysterious irregularity. But late some evening, when you're willing to take a chance, wander down the little alleyway that leads to this upstairs club. When things are in full swing, the music and the dancing go on well into the early morning hours.

Greek Culture

Greek dancing falls into two categories. You can always identify

HOW TO MAKE GREEK COFFEE

Greek coffee is made in a *briki* (select the heaviest one you can find), two servings at a time. The secret of good Greek coffee is timing. Sugar is added during preparation, and the coffee is boiled three times.

You will need: a briki
                200 ml (2/3 cup) cold water
                10 ml (2 tsps) sugar (medium sweet)
                10 ml (2 heaping tsps) Greek coffee

Combine water and sugar in the briki and bring to a boil. Remove from heat and stir in coffee briskly. Return to heat. The coffee will boil again right away. Remove again just before the brown foam overflows. Tap the side of the briki several times with a spoon until the foam subsides.

Return to heat again. Let it boil almost to the top, remove and tap again. Repeat this procedure once more.

Spoon the foam evenly into two demitasse cups. Pour coffee into each cup slowly. Serve immediately.

the *vlachika* country dances by the dominance of the clarinet. These are the slow foot-stomping dances, originally war dances, that depicted the stealthy approach of the Greeks upon their enemies. They reached their highest development during the Turkish occupation when villagers would perform them to express their defiance and determination that Greek culture should continue.

The bouzouki is the instrument of the taverna dances, which originated in the working class restaurants of the nineteenth and early twentieth centuries. Men gathered to eat, drink, talk, and, as the night wore on, dance. These dances are much more concerned with romance and passion and are filled with high stepping jumps.

Folk dancing is very popular with Greek young people, and non-Greeks are welcome to join the many dance groups. For further information, call the Greek Community Centre beside the Church at 266-7148.

Festivals and Holidays

The risen Christ is the focus of the Greek Orthodox Church, and Easter is the most important of all the many Church holidays. The ritual observance of Easter begins with *Apokreas.* Very much like Mardi Gras, this is the last day of feasting and merrymaking before the forty-day Lenten fast begins. The local community has several dinners and dances, which are open to all.

Saturday evening at the stroke of midnight is when the glorious Easter liturgy begins. A replica of Christ's tomb, heaped with fresh gardenias, is carried from the altar through the Church and around the building, followed by hundreds of children each holding a candle. Naturally the Church is packed, so, if you want to witness this very special event, you must come early to get a seat.

Sunday is for feasting. Many families break their fast with *mayerista,* the traditional Easter soup made of lamb's heart and tripe. And look in the bakeries for the braided Easter bread, *lambropsomo,* with several whole red eggs baked into it. On Easter Sunday everyone cracks their red eggs against those of friends. If yours comes out of the battles unscathed, it means good luck.

Greek Independence Day, March 25th, celebrates the date in 1821 when the Greeks freed themselves of their four-hundred-year oppres-

Greek section at Kitsilano Library, 2425 MacDonald.

sion under the Ottoman Turks. The community usually sponsors children's programs and special dinners and dances.

Greeks also celebrate Christmas, but the traditional time for gift-giving is at New Year's. This is the day when the *vassilopita* is cut. Somewhere hidden in this sweetbread is a coin, and the person who gets it will have luck for a whole year. If you want to try it, the local bakeries usually have vassilopita complete with a coin.

After morning church on January 6, at Epiphany, the whole community gathers at Kitsilano Beach for the blessing of the waters. The priest blesses a cross, then tosses it into the waves. Young men then dive into the water, and the one who finds it is acclaimed hero of the day.

As for secular events, if you want a good sampling of Greek home baking, the two-day annual Festival of Food held at the Church in early May is an excellent opportunity to try out sweets and pastries.

The first Greek Days were held in 1974 and became an instant institution. Usually slated for late June, this is simply a time when the Greek community opens its arms to the rest of the city. From noon on Sunday to early the next morning, the Greek section of West Broadway is closed to traffic and it feels like most of Vancouver comes out to eat souvlaki, dance, and slowly stroll the street *peri pato,* in Greek promenade style.

Around Town

There are dozens of Greek restaurants around Vancouver, and, for something different, I would try **Platanos** (2975 Cambie). The decor is not particularly special but the Athenian-style food is. Their *kleftiko* (lamb baked in foil and *fytini*) is an outstanding winter dish. The house specialty is *Giouvetsi Demos.* It's a casserole of beef stewed in tomato sauce and baked in the oven with Greek-style spaghetti.

If you are downtown, visit **Yiannis** at 1642 Robson. The big mural of the Greek Islands covering one wall sets the right tone for enjoying the best saganaki in town. For an entrée, try their slow-cooked village-style roast lamb.

If You Want to Know More

At the Kitsilano Public Library, on MacDonald just near Broadway they have made a special effort to serve the local community, Greek and

143

non-Greek. If you happen to read Greek, there is a good selection of novels and non-fiction, but you don't need to know the language to enjoy the lifestyle magazines from Athens that come into the library each week.

If you are planning to travel, this is the best library branch for books about Greece, and it also has the largest selection of cookbooks. But the best resource is the librarian, Mrs. Sheila Berndorfer, an enthusiast for all things Hellenic. She often puts together special Greek displays, knows the community inside out, and is a strong supporter of the Greek-Canadian association called Pharos, which welcomes non-Greeks to learn about the arts and culture of both ancient and modern Greece through lectures and events. Their local mailing address is Box 2120, Vancouver, B.C. V6B 3TS.

Floka is a sister organization of local Greek poets and writers. Their meetings are conducted in Greek, but the group often sponsors cultural programs for non-Greeks. Call 733-9934 for more information. There are several local Greek newpapers, but only the *Acropolis* has an English section. You can order a subscription from P.O. Box 35417, Station E, Vancouver, V6M 4G5.

If you are going to Greece or are simply curious about learning the language, there are lots of night school courses offered through the Board of Education, although it's probably more fun to take classes offered through the Greek Community Centre. Your kids are welcome to join any of the half dozen after-school Greek language classes held around the city.

Many Vancouver residents have probably already visited one of the restaurants in Greektown. Next time, don't stop there; make it a jumping off point for walking and shopping around one of this city's most colorul and interesting neighborhoods.

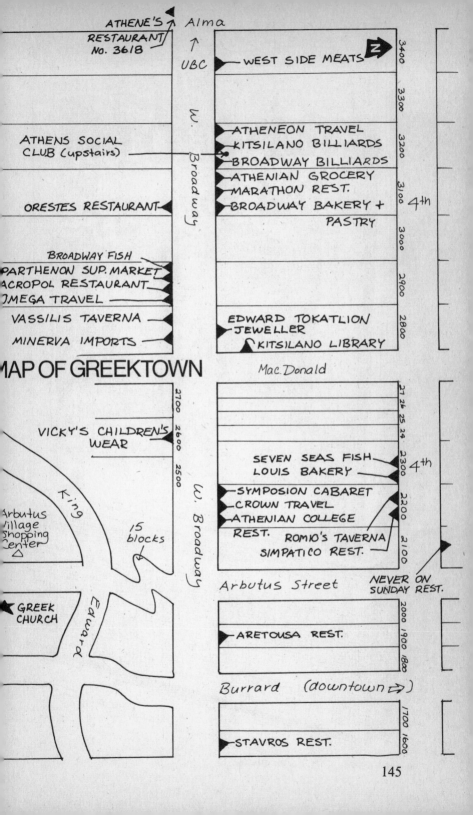

ATHENE'S
RESTAURANT
No. 3618

Alma

UBC

W. Broadway

WEST SIDE MEATS

3400
3300

ATHENEON TRAVEL
KITSILANO BILLIARDS
BROADWAY BILLIARDS

ATHENS SOCIAL
CLUB (upstairs)

ATHENIAN GROCERY
MARATHON REST.
BROADWAY BAKERY +
PASTRY

3200

3100

4th

ORESTES RESTAURANT

3000

BROADWAY FISH
PARTHENON SUP. MARKET
ACROPOL RESTAURANT
OMEGA TRAVEL

2900

VASSILIS TAVERNA

EDWARD TOKATLION
JEWELLER

2800

MINERVA IMPORTS

KITSILANO LIBRARY

MAP OF GREEKTOWN

Mac.Donald

2700

VICKY'S CHILDREN'S
WEAR

2600

2500

King

W. Broadway

27 26 25 24

2300

4th

SEVEN SEAS FISH
LOUIS BAKERY

Arbutus
Village
Shopping
Center

15
blocks

SYMPOSION CABARET
CROWN TRAVEL
ATHENIAN COLLEGE
REST.   ROMIO'S TAVERNA
SIMPATICO REST.

2200

2100

Edward

Arbutus Street

NEVER ON
SUNDAY REST.

GREEK
CHURCH

ARETOUSA REST.

2000 1900 1800

Burrard (downtown ⇨)

STAVROS REST.

1700 1600

145

'La Grotta' at 1791 Commercial

LITTLE ITALY

Although Italian-Canadians live all over the Lower Mainland now, they always come back to Commercial Drive. This is still the place to buy the best fresh pasta and fresh roasted coffee beans; the homemade ice cream can't be beat, the fine Italian leathers are exquisite, and the top-quality imported children's wear is the fanciest you'll find in town.

Commercial Drive is the heart of Little Italy. It is full of life and activity as people stand on the street corners and trade local gossip. Physically, it is one of the most pleasant streets in town—lots of awnings and canopies, huge shade trees down at the north end, and no big parking lots to walk through. And there's lots of variety among all the dozens of little stores, which makes it a window shopper's delight. For a hundred reasons, none of it should be missed.

Italians in Vancouver

The biggest wave of Italian immigrants came after World War II. By that time the community had shifted its center from the Strathcona area east to Grandview Woodlands. Commercial was the main shopping area, but, as the community prospered and grew, business extended along the northern border of Grandview, so that today you can find Italian bakeries, barbers, grocery stores, jewelers, and travel agents not only along Commercial from Broadway to Venables but also east along Hastings from Semlin right to the gates of the Pacific National Exhibition at Renfrew.

Historic Little Italy

There are still some reminders of the first Little Italy, which was located on Keefer, Prior, East Georgia, and Main. In those days Chinatown was much smaller and was located farther west at Pender and Carrall. It was a lively area back in the twenties and thirties when False Creek came right up to Clark Drive and boys used it as a swimming hole. There were a couple of big theaters along Main Street then, the Imperial at Pender and the Empress at East Georgia where the electrical substation now stands. Traveling opera companies used to come to town regularly, and audiences would pack the theaters.

Hogan's Alley, between Union and Prior, north of Main, was the toughest area in town according to legend. It seems there was nothing that didn't happen here—gambling, bootlegging, prostitution, even murder. When Mayor Gerry McGeer decided to clean up the city in 1935, Hogan's Alley disappeared virtually overnight, and now it's only oldtimers who remember.

Strathcona is a Chinese community these days, but some of the first residents and a couple of the original Italian shops are still around—like **Tosi's** at 624 Main Street, with the big wicker-covered wine jugs in the window. With its old wooden floors and mahogany counters Tosi's hasn't changed much from the way it was sixty years ago.

For another trip back in time, visit **Benny's Market.** This grocery and import store, at 598 Union Street, was started by Alphonso Benedetti in 1912 and is still run by the family. Aside from all of the regular Italian foods, this is the one store in town where you can be sure of finding a copy of the excellent book *Opening Doors, Vancouver's East End.* If you want to know about the early ethnic history of Vancouver, this book of personal interviews is the one to get.

Italian Food

There are two basic types of Italian cooking: northern and southern. In the north, where the land is fertile, urbanized, and affluent, the cuisine is more varied and sophisticated, often ranked with French and Chinese as one of the great cuisines of the world. The sauces are light, herbs are used with a delicate hand, and the basic cooking fat is butter.

In the poorer southern region, cheaper ingredients are used. Olive oil is king and gives its distinctive stamp to the robust, highly seasoned dishes that come from the boot of Italy. This is where the ubiquitous tomato sauce comes from and garlic, basil, and oregano are used lavishly. Pasta is found everywhere—the flat noodles, popular in the north, are made with eggs; the pasta of the south is tubular, dried, and eggless.

Ristorantes, Trattorias, and Coffee Bars

Most of the early Italian immigrants came from the rural areas of the south, and it is the hearty styles of Neopolitan and Sicilian cooking that most North Americans are used to. Although many elegant, northern-style *ristorantes* have opened all over Vancouver in recent years, Little Italy is best known for its excellent and authentic southern-style *trattorias* where you can find the best of this cooking. The decor is always minimal—not much more than checked table cloths and candles stuck in wine bottles.

The *caffes* (coffee bars) often double as billiard halls. Like the Greek "kaffenion," these are unofficial social clubs where the men gather to talk and do business. This is the old style of small town life, and most of the Italian women I have talked to don't feel very comfortable in these places, especially alone, as it often means being exposed to comments, whistles, and staring.

The Best Restaurants in Little Italy

Every Italian I have interviewed says the **Gallo Doro** (1736 Commercial) is the best old-style trattoria you'll find in Vancouver. People start lining up here at 11:00 on Friday mornings for their special *frito misto* (literally, mixed fried things). The specialty is deep-fried *calamari* (squid).

When Rino Tessuti opened his first restaurant, **Il Corso,** in the 1500 block Commercial, every woman was personally presented with a single long-stemmed red rose. He and his wife, Lina, have since moved down the street. The new **Cafe Rosticceria** (920 Commercial) specializes in lunchtime pasta. There's no menu here—Signor Tessuti brings you the day's selection of antipasto and a big plate of linguine or fettuccine for your whole table. Recently both the premises and the menu have been expanded to include a full array of fish dishes. Another best bet.

Carlucci's at 2543 East Hastings, is a real find. From the outside you wouldn't guess that there is a large and comfortable trattoria in the back room. Carlucci makes his own pasta daily (you'll pass the kitchen on the way in). Try his cannelloni stuffed with *ricotta* cheese and topped with meat sauce. **Tommy O's** (2590 Commercial) marble and white-tiled, light-filled trattoria is actually owned by Irishman Tommy

149

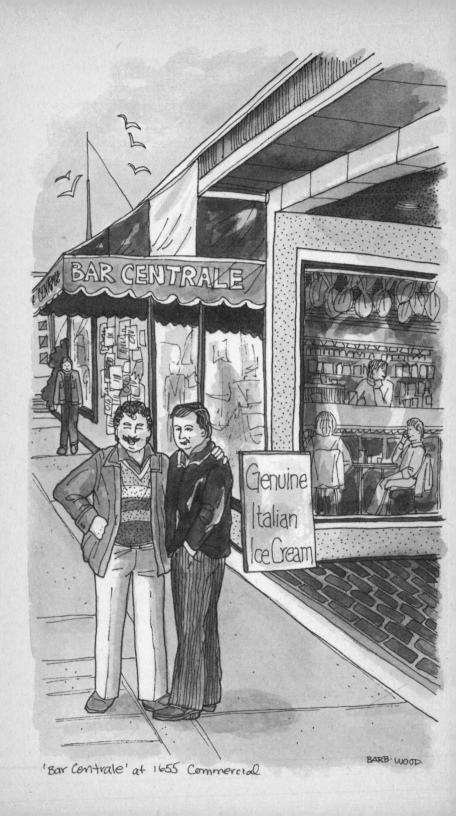

'Bar Centrale' at 1655 Commercial

BARB·WOOD.

O'Brien. His true love for northern-style pasta dishes shows in his superb (best in town) Fettucine Alfredo. For true ristorante dining, try Dario's **La Piazza,** located in the Italian Cultural Centre at 12th and Slocan. The prices can be high, but the food is exquisite. Don't forget to ask about their *pesce frasco del giorno* (fresh fish of the day). You'll also appreciate their extensive list of Italian wines.

The Bar Centrale (1655 Commercial) is one of the friendliest caffes on the Drive and has the best seats for people watching. If it's a sweltering day and you don't want something hot, try one of the Italian soft drinks. The bitter edge of a cold *brio* may be a surprise at first, but it's very refreshing.

At the **Pofi Bar** (1308 Commercial) they put a few chairs and tables out on the sidewalk during the hottest part of the summer. The homemade *gelata* (ice cream) attracts a lot of non-Italians, and rumor has it that **Continental Billiards** (1150 Commercial) has the best cappuccino in town.

Dining and Dancing

The best time to go to **Luigi's Moka Restaurant** (1728 Commercial) is on weekend evenings. Underneath the giant papier maché tree in the middle of the restaurant, a four-piece band gets going sometime after 9:00 p.m., and you can dance the night away to mellow ballads.

The **Gransasso** (1622 Commercial) is a step up, both gastronomically and musically. Here you'll find white tablecloths and a large dance floor. Although many couples stay for the whole evening, you can also drop by for an hour and have just an espresso and a pastry.

A few blocks north at **Orlando's Gondola** (1130 Commercial), Orlando himself gets into the act when he starts on his repetoire of arias often accompanied by his son on accordion.

A Shopping Tour of Little Italy

The Italian stores on Commercial Drive start to pop up north of Broadway around 6th Avenue and continue fourteen blocks down to Venables. The largest concentration of shops is between 3rd and Kitchener.

This retail area has been a going concern since the early teens of the century. In 1911 optimistic local entrepeneurs changed the name of the

ITALIAN FOOD SHOPPING

Canned Lupini Beans Drain and salt. Favourite movie munchies in Italy.

Dried Chestnuts Chew and chew and chew. Another popular snack.

Bottled Pesto Sauce Dilute with milk or wine.

Pickled Eggplant One of many bottled additives for your antipasto plate.

De Cecco and Buitoni The best brands of dried pasta.

Amorini Biscuits The package designs of many imported goods are almost as good as the contents. These are one of dozens of Italian biscuits.

main street from Park to Commercial Drive, and later it became the main thoroughfare for the old Interurban Railway. Some of the city's oldest stores can be found here; Manitoba Hardware, established in 1904, is still going strong, and the old Woolworth store, near 1st Avenue hasn't changed much since 1952.

You can drive or walk to the Hastings shopping strip. Turn east on Venables and then north on Victoria and the Vancouver East Cultural Centre. From there it's five blocks to Hastings. The best shops are between Garden Road, just west of Nanaimo, and Kaslo on the east.

Beyond Spaghetti: A Guide to an Italian Grocery Store

Of all the ethnic food stores, Italian shops are probably the least intimidating to North Americans. But you'll still find lots of things you don't recognize, let alone know what to do with. So here's a little help.

Fresh and dried pasta comes in dozens of shapes and sizes. In Italy there are over two hundred varieties, but the twenty or thirty you will find in Vancouver are more than enough to keep you busy.

Pasta basically goes by size. The very tiny *pastini* ("ini" on the end of a word means it's diminutive)—shells, stars, alphabet letters—are for soups. The ribbons and strings—light pastas like *linguine* and *fettuccine*—and the bowl shapes like *tortellini* go best with cream and butter-based sauces. Little *ziti* and *penne* are usually matched with stronger meat sauces. The big pastas like *cannellone* and long strips of *lasagne* are for baking in casseroles.

Fresh is the best for pasta, but, if you're buying dried, look for de Cecco brand. Not only does it have the most interesting shapes, it's famous among gourmet cooks for the way it absorbs a sauce. Butoni or Barillo are good second choices.

There are dozens of Italian cheeses and every grocery has at least a small selection. Start with a mild *fontina* (it has tiny holes in it) or *gorgonzola*, the reputed "king" of table cheeses—creamy and soft when young, strong like blue cheese when it ages. When it's available, *marscarponi* is another creamy cheese often used in cakes, and for something a bit stronger try *taleggio* made from dry salted curds with a slightly aromatic flavor. Finally, if you're buying parmesan for grating, to get the best quality, make sure it's marked "reggiano."

153

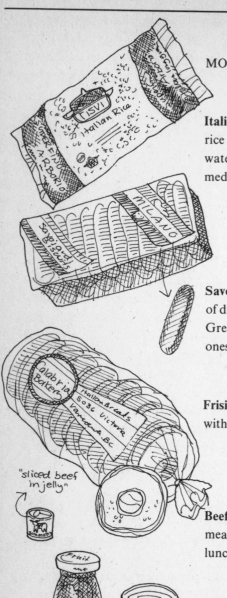

Italian Risotto   For authentic Italian rice dishes, use 200 ml (1½ cups) of water for every 120 ml (1 cup) of this medium grain rice.

Savoiardi Biscuits   One of the dozens of dried biscuits and cookies you'll find. Great with ice cream. Try tiny amaretto ones for coffee time.

Frisini   Delicious crusty bread flavored with fennel seed.

"sliced beef in jelly"

Beef in Jelly   One of the best canned meats you'll find, and a typical Italian lunch meat.

Fruits in Mustard Sauce   Excellent for decorating hams.

Tripe   If you're not ready for cow's stomach yet, try the sauce. Excellent.

154

There are all kinds of processed and cured meats to choose from. *Mortadella* is a pinkish and subtly spiced ground pork loaf from Bologna (the original of bland North American baloney). *Capocollo* is a cold cut made from the pig's neck. Marbled with fat, it comes hot and hotter. The brighter the orange spices on the outside, the stronger it is. *Prosciutto* is exquisite. This ham is very delicately cured and eaten raw, and it must be cut in paper thin slices. Though it's almost sweet enough for dessert, prosciutto is one of the classic antipasto meats served before the main meal with melons or fresh figs.

The big pieces of dried flattened white fish are called *baccala* (salted cod) or *stoccafisso* (if it's unsalted). Both must be soaked for at least twenty-four hours. There are dozens of ways to prepare baccala; one of the easiest is Florentine-style dredged in flour, lightly fried, and topped with a fresh tomato sauce.

The grocery stores seem to leave fresh vegetables to the super-markets (artichokes, eggplants, and, of course, tomatoes are the Italian favorites), but occasionally you will see a basket of what looks like cut-off bulbs from celery bunches. This is anise-flavored *finoccio*. You can slice it up, add dressing, and serve finoccio as a salad, or dip pieces into a dish of good olive oil with about three centimeters of salt in the bottom.

Bertolli and Tiger Brand get the highest rating among Italian olive oils, but many cooks claim that the oil for export is second-rate and prefer the heavier and more flavorful Greek oils, which are carried in all the stores.

If you have overindulged a bit, a thimbleful of *digestivo* is what you need. Artichoke is the most common, though you'll see half a dozen different flavors. The alcoholic content is probably what makes you feel better. Not surprisingly, a spoonful before dinner does wonders for the appetite.

Finally, if the price of Perrier has got you down, make your own mineral water with Frizzina. In Europe the table water tastes so bad that many families perk it up with these little sachets of sodium bicarbonate and tartaric acid.

The Prince of Pasta

There's a rumor that the pope blessed Peter Olivieri's ravioli machine before he opened his store at 3rd and Commercial in 1957.

GNOCCHI

Gnocchi is a relative of pasta, and it's always served as a first course. It's usually made with flour and potato, but here we're using ricotta cheese and spinach.

You will need: 2 kilograms (4 pounds) of spinach
450 grams (1 pound) of ricotta cheese
5 spoonfuls of grated parmesan
3 egg yolks
melted butter
flour
salt

Boil spinach uncovered in salted water. When cooked, wash with cold water, strain thoroughly, and chop finely.

In a bowl mix the ricotta, egg yolks, parmesan, and a little salt. Add chopped spinach, and mix again.

Take a small spoonful of the mixture and roll into the gnocchi shape. Then roll in flour.

Drop the gnocchis in boiling water. Cook three to four minutes until the gnocchi rises to the surface. Remove with a slotted spoon, and drain.

Spoon melted butter over the gnocchis and sprinkle with parmesan.

Serve hot.

True or not, his pasta certainly has a touch of the divine. **Olivieri's** carries all the standard Italian groceries, but the real gold is at the back of the store. Here you can choose from a tray of freshly made ribbonlike egg or green spinach fettuccine, stuffed bellybutton tortellinis, meat or cheese *ravioli*, and little *raviolinis*. Olivieri's also dries their own pasta, which you can find in plastic bags at the front of the store.

Pesto is a classic pasta sauce made with basil, pine nuts, oil, and garlic. Olivieri's house brand is excellent, especially when reworked with a little milk. His clam sauce is also good, and is even better with a little white wine and lemon juice.

Breads and Sweets

Most of the grocery stores stock bread from two of the local Italian bakeries, **Fortuna** (2209 Springer) in Burnaby and **Calabria** (5036 Victoria Drive). I am particularly partial to Calabria's pizza bread, but, best of all, I like the *frisini* made by both places. Round, crusty, and flavored with whole fennel seeds, they definitely succeed when slathered with butter. The authentic Italian way is to drizzle frisini slices with olive oil and sprinkle with a little oregano.

For fresh bread made on the spot, try **Renato's** bakery at the corner of 2nd and Commercial. Italian bread is made the same way as French bread, but shaped into a big flattened ball. This place also has Italian baguettes and an excellent dry fruit loaf called *jambella*.

At **Carmelo's Pastry Shop** (1403 Commercial) you can find homemade brioches. They look just like croissants (in fact, they're often called croissants), but an Italian brioche is sweeter and heavier. This is the place to make your sweet tooth happy. Carmello is also a painter (you'll see some of his work on the wall), and his artistry shows in his elaborately decorated cakes. You can put an order in for his special *santonoré*—cream puffs filled with vanilla or chocolate custard and slathered with fresh whipped cream. For an extra treat, try Carmelo's individual hand-dipped chocolates.

Veal and Homemade Sausages

There are several Italian butchers on Commercial Drive, all used to dealing with special requests. They will pound medallions of milk-fed veal flat for delicate *scallopine* dishes, or cut up the shanks for tender *ossobuco*. At **Falcone Brothers** (1810 Commercial) they take pride in

Sausage making at
Falcone Bros.
1810 Commercial Drive.

grinding their beef for delicate meat sauces, and, every Monday and Thursday, they make fresh pork sausages right in the front of the store. At **Perri Meat Market** (1439 Commercial), the oldest butcher on the Drive, they also make their own *salsicce*. Salsicce are especially good served with *polenta*, a type of cornmeal cake or bread that is a staple of the northern diet. On their own, they can be fried or barbecued and served with a sprinkle of lemon juice.

More on Cheese

For the best selection of cheese on the Drive and one of the best atmospheres anywhere in Little Italy, don't miss **La Grotta Del Formaggio** (1791 commercial). Huge rope-wrapped *provolones* hang in the window and, if you're at all unsure of what you want, Frank Calla and his partner, Brucesi Fortunata, always offer to let you taste first.

For the freshest ricotta cheese in western Canada head for **Scardillo's** (1670 Commercial Drive). This family business also whole-sales their partly-skimmed mozarella throughout Alberta and B.C.

Beans and Machines

If you're coming from the north, one of your first stops should be **Coloiera's** (2206 Commercial). The shop has been going strong for eleven years now, mainly because Mrs. Coloiera roasts her own coffee beans and wholesales her blends to many of the best Italian restaurants in town. If you want to try before you buy, there are a few small tables in front where you can sit with a cappuccino and the morning paper.

For making your own Italian-style coffee, the **Espresso Cappuccino Coffee Machine Company** (2085 Commercial) has all the necessary apparatus. Because the machinery to produce steamed milk is fairly elaborate, cappuccino machines are expensive; they start at a hundred dollars. Aside from coffee-makers, this shop also stocks fancy electric pasta makers that do it all for you right from scratch. For smaller Italian kitchen machines like noodle cutters, ravioli trays, and food mills, try the local grocery stores for the best buys.

A Little Vino

The Liquor Control Board store at 1520 Commercial makes a special effort to meet local demand and stocks a good selection of

159

'La Bottega' at 1616 Commercial

ITALIAN IMPORTS

Italian children are always beautifully dressed and if you have any bambinos to shop for try **La Bottega,** one of the original Italian stores on Commercial Drive. It stocks fine linen and giftware as well as top quality children's wear from Italy. The fanciest dresses and suits are for christenings and confirmations.

Italian products. Rubesco Lungarotti, Rifosco Grave del Fuili, Bertolli Orvieto, and Bolla Soave are very popular and reasonably priced wines.

Brolio Vencento is a sweet dessert wine that you don't find in many places. The store also brings in Sambuca, an Italian licorice liqueur. Italians usually prefer red wines with food. White wines are preferred as aperitifs to sip before the meal.

La Bella Figura

Italians are famous for their sense of fashion and cutting a fine figure. For adults (and children), Commercial Drive has the best shoe stores in Vancouver. The fashions are very high at **Amorelli's** (1432 Commercial)—lots of stiletto heels and pointy toes—and so are the prices, but the feel of real Italian leather may soften the blow. At **Kalena** (1526 Commercial) the styles of both men's and women's shoes are a little more subdued, and so are the price tags. Watch for their excellent January and July sales.

At Melonari's (1301 Commercial) you're in for a pleasant surprise. Mr. and Mrs. Melonari make their own shoes in their nearby factory on Parker St. with Italian leather and using Italian designs. However because they don't have to pay import costs their prices are naturally much lower. Melonari's also fills custom orders.

For women's clothing, the oldest store on the Drive is **Bunny's Key to Fashion** (1470 Commercial). The shop doesn't particularly specialize in Italian imports, though the selection is fashionable and moderately priced. But Bunny herself is a Commercial Drive original; everybody gets special attention, and she's always ready to drop business for a chat and a glass of wine.

The Italian tailors on Commercial Drive are known right across Canada for their fine custom workmanship. Renzo's has recently moved to new premises at 1684 Commercial but Angelo's has been in the same spot at 1501 Commercial for many years. For the classiest lines of ready to wear try L'uomo Vogue at 1390 Commercial Drive.

Records and Gifts

Italians come from all over the Pacific Northwest for the excellent selection at **Ital Records** (1409 Commercial). Young people enjoy the more modern pop singers, but the best sellers are the romantic Neapolitan folk songs presented by artists like Guiseppe de Stafano and Lucano Taoli.

Tevere's — 2565 E. Hastings

REGIONAL GROCERS

There are half a dozen Italian grocery stores along the East Hastings border of Grandview Woodlands. Many of the older local residents go shopping every day and have patronized the same store for years because the owner comes from their region of Italy.

Ital Records was also the first gift store on the Drive. The gifts and knicknacks in this store are typical of what you will find on Commercial Drive—very rococco and lots of gold leaf. If you want something simpler, the coffee sets are often very elegant, sometimes with a pricetag to match.

Little Italy Part II

The shopping district along the northern border of Little Italy on East Hastings is almost undiscovered by non-Italians, and it's well worth a visit.

All of the stores have an old-fashioned flavor and a strong neighborhood feel. There are half a dozen food stores, including a branch of **Scardillos** (2580 East Hastings) and the large and airy **Falesca Italian Center** (2341 East Hastings), where you can buy imported Italian vegetable seeds in the spring. At **Tevere's** (2565 East Hastings) you can find a marvelous array of boxed Italian chocolates and a counter full of hard candies. Ask to try some of the chocolate-toffee *rossanas*. Several big glass jars are filled with oval-shaped white and pastel *confettis*. You will find these candies in almost every store, and they are traditionally passed around at celebrations.

The exquisitely crafted children's shoes at **Sabrina's** (2365 East Hastings) are tempting, and **Rose's** (2400 East Hastings) has fine imported clothes for youngsters. The inside doorway leads to **La Rinascente** (2401 East Hastings), jampacked with elaborate Italian furniture. At the **Linens and Gift Imports** (2533 East Hastings) you'll find the area's biggest selection of china and knicknacks.

Firenza Fine Arts (2584 East Hastings) has a beautiful selection of earrings for pierced ears. The owner claims that Italian craftsmen use seventy-five percent of the world's jewelry gold. For Italian magazines, comics, and cookbooks, try **Emma Marian** (2330 East Hastings).

Finally, a special mention goes to **Bosa's,** located at 562 Victoria drive between the Hastings and Commercial shopping areas. This is one of the oldest and best stocked of all the Italian food stores. It also gets a recommendation for the high quality and low prices of its fresh meat.

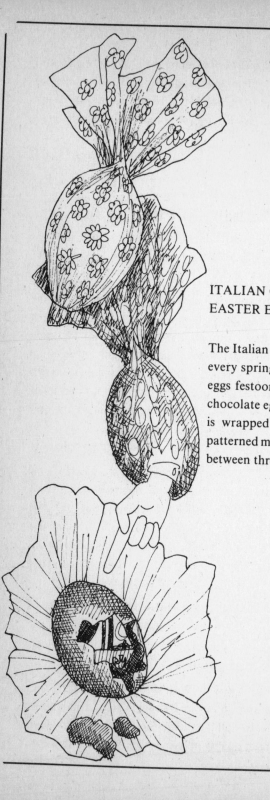

ITALIAN CHOCOLATE EASTER EGGS

The Italian food stores are transformed every spring by dozens of fancy Easter eggs festooned from the ceilings. Each chocolate egg (with a little prize inside) is wrapped in a huge sheet of fancy patterned metallic paper. They're priced between three and ten dollars.

Italian Culture

Completed in 1976, the **Italian Cultural Centre** is located outside the main shopping area at 12th and Slocan. Nevertheless, this large facility ties the community together, providing social services to families and a place for meetings, festivals, exhibitions, and small concerts. The Centro shows Italian movies every month; your children are welcome to join the young people's choir and learn Italian and Spanish songs (the teacher is bilingual). There's also a library here—filled with gorgeous art books donated by the Italian government.

The Cultural Centre operates on a tight budget, and most of its advertising is by word of mouth. However, at the time of writing, a monthly newsletter was being instituted, which you can receive by phoning 430-3337 or writing 3075 Slocan.

Many of the special programs at the Centre are sponsored by the dozen or so Italian clubs in Vancouver (each representing a different region of the country) or in conjunction with the **Italian Cultural Institute.** The Institute (688-0809) is funded by the Italian government and, in the past couple of years, has arranged a wide variety of events ranging from a visit by the Sicilian Puppet Company to a workshop with the famous Italian pacifist Danilo Dolci.

The Italian Canadian Sports Federation also has its offices in the Cultural Centre. You can see some of the best soccer games in town every weekend in the adjacent park and in the grassy field behind the **Brittania Community Centre** at Commercial and Napier.

Festivals and Holidays

For Italians, Easter is the biggest celebration of the year. It begins forty days early with *Carnevale*. Just like the Mardi Gras, this is the last opportunity to eat, drink, and generally make merry before the Lenten fast begins.

Carnevale is celebrated over two days at the Italian Cultural Centre. There are food booths all day, and there is dancing in the evening. If anything funny happens, remember that this is the time of year when practical jokes are allowed. Throughout the weekend huge puppet heads are paraded throughout the hall—double life-size paper mache models of important and famous people.

At Easter time every household will have a *columba* now sold

Italian Days on Commercial Drive.

year-round in the grocery stores. The boxed cakes with the dove on the front are made in the shape of a bird. They represent the risen spirit of Christ. These dry coffee cakes will keep for several months.

There are several Italian churches in Vancouver. In the heart of Little Italy, at **St. Francis of Assisi** (1020 Semlin), mass is given in Italian. Traditionally, at Easter, very religious people will bring a little basket of eggs to be blessed by the priest. At home, the family ritually eats one of the sanctified eggs.

Christmas is not as big a celebration as Easter, but every family will have a *panetone* on their table Christmas morning. This is the other boxed cake you'll see in the food stores. It is very much like a columba, except the panetone has raisins and is shaped like a small mountain with a flat top. Both these imported cakes are expensive—usually over ten dollars—but I find them quite addicting, especially with lots of butter.

At the beginning of June, the Cultural Centre is busy again with the *Festa de la Republica,* which celebrates the unification of the Italian states. In late June or early July Commercial Drive gears up for Italian Days. On Sunday the street is closed to traffic and the whole east end comes out for a good time at the Italian Market. The shops are all open; there's lots of good red wine and barbecued sausages. The Italian bands get the dancing started, and in the afternoon *bocce* experts demonstrate how to play this European style of lawn bowling.

Around Town

For more Italian coffee, try the beans at **Faema** (106 East Broadway). Their selection of sophisticated coffee makers and pasta machines from Italy seems limitless. They even have special Italian ice cream makers.

There are a number of *gelati* (Italian ice cream) parlors in Vancouver, like the stylish **Ping Pong** (1129 Robson). My favorite Italian gourmet raves about the fresh fruit ice cream at the **Rialto** (855 Denman Street), but I like coming back to the **Venezia** (5752 Victoria), the first such place in town. The decor is a lot plainer, but the old man who runs the place doesn't mind if you linger. He says his Venetian-style ice cream recipe is a family secret (it's got something to do with the milk). In fact, Victoria Drive has a number of Italian shops. Try the jam-packed **Albi Grocery** (5487 Victoria), and for meats the **Calabria**

(5036 Victoria) has all the Italian cuts as well as handling everything else from Chinese duck eggs to goat meat for Indian cooking.

Monte Cristo Jewelers, (5733 Victoria Drive), handles some of the beautiful coral pieces popular with Italians. And as one of the owners suggested, don't be shy about trying a little bargaining.

If You Want to Know More

L'Eco d'Italia has been serving the Italian community for a long time. Unfortunately, the weekly newspaper is in Italian. However, the local community paper, the *Highland Echo*, covers a lot of the local Italian news in English and can keep you posted on what's happening.

With over fifty thousand Italians in the Lower Mainland, the Italian phone book is as much a necessity as a luxury. For non-Italians, the many ads are an excellent shopping guide. You can pick it up free in most stores in the area.

The Britannia Community Centre has a good stock of Italian books and magazines in the library. They also have Italian puppet shows, and, during Italian Days in the summer, they decorate the Centre and sponsor many different demonstrations.

If you want to learn Italian, you're not alone. Many Italians do too. Each region has a distinct dialect, and a woman from Calabria may not be able to communicate with someone from Abruzzi. Many of the Italian classes in Vancouver are attended by immigrants anxious to learn a common language. Both the school at Britannia and the Italian Cultural Centre coordinate a wide variety of Italian language programmes. Britannia offers beginner classes, while the courses at the Cultural Centre are usually a little more advanced and make use of an excellent language lab. Italian is a beautiful language and is not very difficult to learn.

Whether you want to do a little serious window shopping or just can't wait another moment for some Italian ice cream, nothing lifts your spirits like a stroll down Commercial Drive. The only problem is that you might never want to go home. Try it and see if I'm not right.

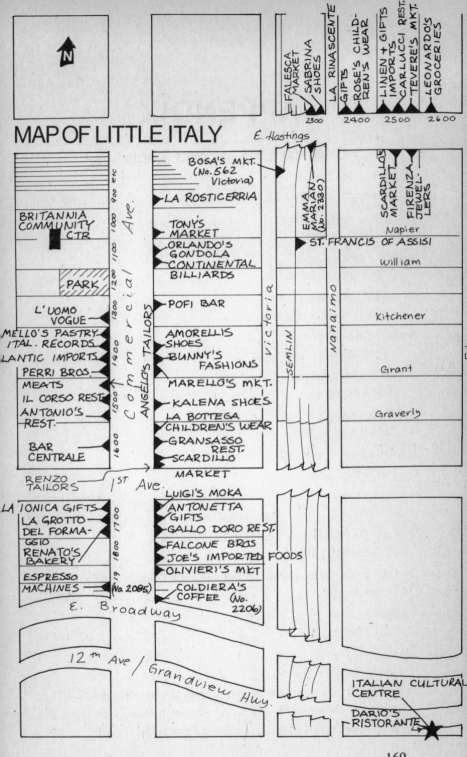

MAP OF LITTLE ITALY

APPENDIX

Cultural Groups and Societies

Asian Studies Center
University of British Columbia Campus 228-4686

Chinese Cultural Center
50 East Pender 687-0729

Hindu Temple
3885 Albert, Burnaby 299-5922

Ismaili Community Society
7900B Alderbridge Way 273-9722

Italian Cultural Center
3075 Slocan 430-3337

Italian Cultural Institute
1200 Burrard 688-0809

Japanese Canadian Citizens Association
475 Alexander 254-7838

Khalsa Diwan Society/Ross St. Sikh Temple
8000 Ross 324-2010

Muslim Mosque
Richmond... 270-3052

Tonari Gumi (Japanese Community Volunteers)
573 East Hastings 255-2651

St. Geroge's Greek Orthodox Church/Greek Community Center
4500 Arbutus 266-7148

Strathcona Community Center
601 Keefer 254-9496

Folk Fest If you want to immerse yourself in the cultural activities of other groups, the annual Folk Fest celebration is your opportunity. For the last two weeks of June and continuing over the Canadian holiday on July 1st, all of the ethnic groups hold open houses, and at Robson Square in downtown Vancouver there is a continuing program of folk dancing demonstrations.   736-1512

The Vancouver Multicultural Society   If you want to learn more about the history and culture of ethnic groups in the community, this society is a good one to get in touch with. The society has active standing committees, which deal with issues in such areas as education and human rights.   731-4647

INDEX

Foreign words and page references to illustrations are italicized.

175